Sedaris

Sedaris

Kevin Kopelson

University of Minnesota Press
Minneapolis • London

This book was made possible in part through the generous support of The Rockefeller Foundation Bellagio Study and Conference Center.

Published by the University of Minnesota Press
111 Third Avenue South, Suite 290
Minneapolis, MN 55401-2520
http://www.upress.umn.edu

Printed in the United States of America on acid-free paper

Library of Congress Cataloging-in-Publication Data

Kopelson, Kevin, 1960–
    Sedaris / Kevin Kopelson.
        p. cm.
    Includes bibliographical references.
    ISBN: 978-0-8166-5084-2; ISBN-10: 0-8166-5084-5 (hc) (acid-free paper) — ISBN: 978-0-8166-5085-9; ISBN-10: 0-8166-5085-3 (pb) (acid-free paper)
    1. Sedaris, David. 2. Sedaris, David—Family. 3. Satire—History and criticism. 4. Autobiography in literature. 5. Self in literature. I. Title.
    PS3569.E314Z75 2007
    818'.5402—dc22
    [B]

                                    2007009516

The University of Minnesota is an equal-opportunity educator and employer.

12 11 10 09 08 07   10 9 8 7 6 5 4 3 2 1

For Adam, Keaton,
Seth, and Sam

I tried listening to *The Misanthrope* and *Fontaine's Fables,* but they were just too dense for me. I'm much too lazy to make that sort of effort. Besides, if I wanted to hear people speaking wall-to-wall French, all I had to do was remove my headphones and participate in what is known as "real life."

—David Sedaris, "The Tapeworm Is In"

Mais où sommes-nous, au juste, quand nous masturbons? Et qui sommes-nous? Qui, en écrivant? Ou plutôt qui faisons-nous semblant d'être?

But where are we, really, when we masturbate? And who are we? Who when we write? Who, rather, are we pretending to be?

—Mireille Dujardin,
Lesbian Lacemakers of the Middle Ages

Contents

David 1

Aunt Monie 7

Lou 17

Sharon 27

Henry 47

Paul 65

Mrs. Colgate 73

Alisha 89

Martin I 111

Martin II 151

Uncle Money 169

Hugh 193

[Your Name Here] 223

Literary Interpolations

André 233

Eve 239

Works by David Sedaris 251

References 255

David

Sedaris calls himself an asshole—not to mention scumbag, shithead, and son of a bitch. Or various characters do. A sister calls the future essayist an asshole at summer camp ("I Like Guys" 88). Then a student does ("The Learning Curve" 88). Then a neighbor does ("The Girl Next Door" 116). Not that Sedaris is the only satirist to deprecate himself. The British poets John Donne (1572–1631) and Alexander Pope (1688–1744), for example, acknowledge their own failings along with those of primary targets. (Donne: "We doe but reprehend those things, which we ourselves have done" [7: 408].) Sedaris, however, is primarily autobiographical—not to mention hilarious, brutally honest, and painfully sad. By reviewing roles he's played in life as well as roles others have played with him, he reveals in alarming detail how he managed to become an asshole. Clearly though, and this has a lot to do with why most of us *like* Sedaris, he's trying to do something about that development—compensation made possible by the fact that some of those roles have shaped his work as an artist.

By calling Sedaris a satirist, I mean to endorse Samuel Johnson's distinction: the writer who "censures" either folly or vice (219). Such writing, of course, is moralistic. The censure, in effect, says, "Shame on you"—much as self-deprecation, or confession, says, "Shame on me." Satire, moreover, represents not so much a genre as a literary mode. Comedy, for example, may contain satire. Think of *Seinfeld* (1989–98), with Jerry, Elaine, and George as comic—or relatively three-dimensional—but Kramer or Newman as satiric (two-dimensional). So can tragedy. Think of *Hamlet,* with Polonius as satiric.

By calling Sedaris a satirist, I also mean to endorse another distinction: the sanguine satirist as opposed to the cynical one. The sanguine satirist likes people. "He tells the truth with a smile, so that he will not repel but cure them of that ignorance which is their worst fault. Such is Horace [Roman poet, 65–8 BC]." Such, for that matter, is Sedaris. The cynical satirist dislikes people. "His aim therefore is not to cure, but to wound, to punish, to destroy. Such is Juvenal [Roman poet, AD 60–131]" (Highet 235). Such, once again, is Sedaris—at least insofar as he targets himself. *Asshole,* after all, expresses not amusement but contempt.

My own target—or goal—is to articulate why many of us not so much like as *love* Sedaris. Love him, no doubt, far more than we do less autobiographical—indeed, less confessional—writers. (The reason Sedaris does something about having become an asshole is of course that he's *ashamed.* Nowadays, though, he's been writing "animal stories." Fables, that is, morality tales like those of Aesop or maybe Jean de La Fontaine. Or so he told me over coffee in Des Moines.) To articulate that, I have to explain who Sedaris is being—and what he's doing—with readers. And the best way for me to do that isn't to say who I or even other critics think he's "really" been or what we think he's done in earlier, less imaginary relationships. It's to say who or what Sedaris himself thinks he has. So—relying in large part on the nonfiction of *Barrel Fever* (1994), *Naked* (1997), *Holidays on Ice* (1997), *Me Talk Pretty One Day* (2000), and *Dress Your Family in Corduroy and Denim* (2004)—I'll schematize, in more or less chronological order, those roles I mentioned: grandparent, parent, sibling, and so on. The most important ones, not surprisingly, will turn out to have been either parental or instructional. I'll use both extensive quotation and paraphrase—something, I confess, my own students aren't allowed. I'll compare that nonfiction, comprising the bulk of those collections, to fiction therein. (Even otherwise shameless writers need masks—literary alter egos—to reveal certain truths. They need, at times, to lie.) And I'll compare Sedaris to Marcel Proust (French novelist, 1871–1922). (Another comparison might be to Lytton Strachey [British biographer, 1880–1932].) Like Sedaris, Proust was gay, mother-minded, satirical, autobiographical, a bit of a slacker, hilarious, and sad. (Proust as alter ego.) Unlike Sedaris, however, Proust was verbose. Whereas "I Like Guys," for example, is under fourteen pages, *Remembrance of Things Past* (1913–27), in English translation, is over four thousand. (Not alter ego but evil twin.) Proust, moreover, was dishonest. His narrator, also named "Marcel," isn't gay. Proust was Parisian too—something Sedaris, despite having moved there and tried to learn the language, will never be.

If Sedaris is gay, however, *Sedaris* the book is not. It's not, that is, the kind of "queer"—or deconstructive—interpretation my first ones represent. (*Love's Litany* [1994] concerned "the writing of modern homoerotics"—from Oscar Wilde to Roland Barthes [French critic, 1915–1980].

Beethoven's Kiss [1996] concerned "pianism, perversion, and the mastery of desire"—from Liszt to Liberace. *The Queer Afterlife of Vaslav Nijinsky* [1997]—well, the title speaks for itself.) It's humanist, rather, much like my last book. (*Neatness Counts* [2004] concerns the poetics of work space, or what Barthes called protocols of literary creation.) Why humanist? Partly because no deconstructor really believes in "text" alone, or in what Barthes called "the death of the author." But mainly because, as with Sedaris and his mother, I've been mourning the death of my father. And unlike all those books, this one— this *essay*, rather—is meant for the general or nonacademic reader in general, for the Sedaris reader in particular. In other words, it's for someone Sedaris might call a snob. Or if not Sedaris, then his mother. Why? Partly because I've been dealing with a rather different, rather difficult mother. (Sharon's alter ego.) But mainly because of a role I myself now play—in life. One, moreover, that shapes my own work. For not only have I been teaching queer theory, critical theory, and cultural studies—mostly to undergraduates. And not only have I been teaching both satire and confession. I've also been helping my partner, David, raise sons Adam (now twenty), Seth (nineteen), and Sam (sixteen). In other words, I, too, have become a father. Or mother perhaps, though Sam—a *Sedaris* dedicatee, as well as its primary, nonimaginary addressee—calls me an elf.

Like all those books, however, *Sedaris* is both autobiographical and "performative." It's autobiographical in that I'm now dealing with my mother in print, if only indirectly. It's performative in that I both address and *situate* the general reader, much as Sedaris does. I situate you, that is, as someone in need of nurture or instruction. It's performative in that by coming out as a fan—in "[Your Name Here]"—I suggest that I, too, have been if not instructed then nurtured by Sedaris. It's performative, moreover, in that you may compare Sedaris prose with that of either Proust or Kopelson, noticing in particular that I refuse to compete. Why? Partly because, as a writer, as a teacher, and even as the youngest of five (four boys, one girl), it's time for me to stop showing off. It's time, that is, to renounce a certain style—a certain selfish virtuosity. But mainly because I couldn't possibly beat him. In fact, I couldn't even tie.

Of course, let's be honest. Any such performativity should speak for itself. I really shouldn't have to articulate those protocols of *reading*. It's just that if I don't, lazy academics—and shame on them—might dismiss *Sedaris* as, well, little more than a book report. But enough of my own deprecation, both self-directed (sanguine) and otherwise (cynical). For it's time, now, to address the question: Why *do* we love Sedaris? And why, for that matter, does he seem to love us back?

Aunt Monie

Sedaris had almost no contact with his maternal grandfather, about whom we're told something awful:

> My mother was sixteen years old when she
> stood on her front porch and watched as men in
> actual white coats carried her father kicking and
> screaming to their local psychiatric hospital, where
> he received a total of thirty-seven electroshock
> treatments. He had been suffering from the D.T.'s,
> a painful hallucinatory state marking an advanced
> stage of alcoholism. My mother visited him every
> day, and often he had no idea who she was. Once,
> thinking she was a nurse, he attempted to slip his
> hand under her skirt. The experience left her with
> a certain haunted quality I very much admired.
> ("Dix Hill" 74)

The source of this information must have been Sharon, the mother. Nor had he much contact with this woman's own mother, about whom we're also told something awful:

When I was fourteen years old, I was sent to spend ten days with my maternal grandmother in western New York State. She was a small and private woman named Billie, and though she never came right out and asked, I had the distinct impression she had no idea who I was. It was the way she looked at me, squinting through her glasses while chewing on her lower lip. That, coupled with the fact that she never once called me by name. "Oh," she'd say, "are you still here?" She was just beginning her long struggle with Alzheimer's disease, and each time I entered the room, I felt the need to reintroduce myself and set her at ease. "Hi, it's me. Sharon's boy, David. I was just in the kitchen admiring your collection of ceramic toads." ("Remembering My Childhood on the Continent of Africa" 197)

He'd even less contact with the paternal grandfather, who died when Sedaris was six. We're told he was morose, but that's almost all we can be told. Unlike Sharon, the man's own son isn't talking—possibly out of a sense of "loyalty," possibly because there's "nothing to report." Nor, despite ample opportunity, did his equally morbid widow— Ya Ya—ever talk. When asked anything about Papou— questions mostly along the lines of, "After he died, did he crap in his pants?"—all she'd say was, "He go to Jesus now" ("Get Your Ya-Ya's Out!" 37). I say ample opportunity because Lou, the father, had Ya Ya move in when she broke her hip—an invasion that drove Sharon herself to drink. While there, this grandmother spoiled Sedaris:

My brother and I came to view our Ya Ya as a primitive version of an ATM machine. She was always good for a dollar or two, and because we were boys, all we had to do was open her car door or inform her the incense had just set fire to one of her embroidered cushions. I'd learned never to accompany her in public, but aside from that, Ya Ya and I had no problem. I saw her as a benign ghost, silent and invisible until you needed a little spending money. ("Get Your Ya-Ya's Out!" 29–30)

The girls saw her as a witch. (Sedaris has four sisters—Lisa, Gretchen, Amy, and Tiffany—and just one brother, Paul.) But the spoiling did nothing to nurture the boys. Like Billie, who "had no idea who I was," not to mention Billie's husband, who had no idea who Sharon was, Ya Ya was too distracted—too haunted, in fact—by her own problems (awful marriage, lonely widowhood) to pay anyone else real attention.

Luckily, another widow both spoiled and nurtured them: great-aunt Mildred, who in private Sharon called "Monie" (*money* plus *moaning*). Not only did this woman have some idea who they were, she "was incredibly perceptive" as well, at least as far as Sedaris was concerned ("Monie Changes Everything" 65). She perceived, for example, a tendency to lie. The first thing she gave him, at about six, was a marionette. "This is Pinocchio," Aunt Monie said. "His nose is long from telling lies. Is that something *you* like to do from time to time, tell little lies?" This, unfortunately, was done with family there, in public, and so was somewhat abusive. Monie also perceived a tendency to kid himself. The last thing she gave Sedaris, about ten years later, was a bearskin rug. This, thankfully, was done in private:

> Alone with my bear on the very first night,
> I double-locked the door and lay upon it naked, the
> way people sometimes did in magazines. I'd hoped
> this might be the best feeling in the world, the
> conquered fur against my bare flesh, but my only

sensation was a creeping uneasiness. Someone was watching me, not a neighbor or one of my sisters, but Aunt Monie's second husband, the one I had seen in the portrait. From the neck up he closely resembled Teddy Roosevelt, the wire-rimmed glasses glinting above a disfiguring walrus mustache. The man had stalked wildebeest across the sizzling veldt and now his predatory eye fell upon me: an out-of-shape seventeen-year-old with oversize glasses and a turquoise studded bracelet, cheapening the name of big-game hunting with his scrawny, pimpled butt. It was an unpleasant image and so it stayed with me a long, long time. (56, 71, emphasis original)

"Unpleasant," and somewhat shameful. The rug, that is, made Sedaris feel a bit foolish; the Pinocchio, a bit vicious. And while Sedaris doesn't get vexed about foolishness anymore—he's come to appreciate that other people "aren't foolish as much as they are kind" ("The Incomplete Quad" 152)—vice does bother him.

Now, of the many things it takes to be vicious—to be an asshole, as it were—the so-called deadliest are anger, greed, lust, sloth, envy, gluttony, and pride. Like François de La Rochefoucauld (1613–1680), Sedaris takes sloth, along with selfishness, to be the worst of these. The two, they feel, comprise the basis of all bad conduct—as well as that of some good. Where La Rochefoucauld called sloth the most "violent" and "malign" of the passions (630), Sedaris recalls having realized, for example, that cafeteria coworkers' habit of leaving steaks "to blacken on the grill as [they] crept off to the stockroom to smoke and play cards or sometimes have sex" was attributable to laziness ("Dinah, the Christmas Whore" 108). And where the moral philosopher wrote of selfishness that "[n]othing is

so vehement as its desires, nothing so concealed as its
aims, nothing so devious as its methods" (563), the essayist worries that even an apology for selfishness can be selfish. (See "Repeat After Me" 141–56.)

Proust, channeling La Rochefoucauld, treats selfishness with characteristic irony: "It is the propitious miracle of self-esteem that, since few of us can have brilliant
connections or profound attainments, those to whom they
are denied still believe themselves to be the best endowed of men, because the optics of our social perspective
make every grade of society seem the best to him who
occupies it and who regards as less favored than himself, ill-endowed, to be pitied, the greater men whom he
names and calumniates without knowing them, judges
and despises without understanding them" (2: 478). He
treats sloth that way too. To quote one paragraph on
Marcel's failure to write *Remembrance of Things Past*—
and all such units, in Proust, are this "symphonic" (Koestenbaum 105):

Had I been less firmly resolved upon settling
down definitively to work, I should perhaps have
made an effort to begin at once. But since my
resolution was explicit, since within twenty-four
hours, in the empty frame of the following day
where everything was so well arranged because
I myself was not yet in it, my good intentions
would be realized without difficulty, it was better
not to start on an evening when I felt ill-prepared.
The following days were not, alas, to prove more
propitious. But I was reasonable. It would have
been puerile, on the part of one who had waited
now for two years, not to put up with a postpone-
ment of two or three days. Confident that by the
day after tomorrow I should have written several

pages, I said not a word more to my parents of my
decision; I preferred to remain patient for a few
hours and then to bring to a convinced and
comforted grandmother a sample of work that was
already under way. Unfortunately the next day was
not that vast, extraneous expanse of time to which
I had feverishly looked forward. When it drew to a
close, my laziness and my painful struggle to
overcome certain internal obstacles had simply
lasted twenty-four hours longer. And at the end of
several days, my plans not having matured, I had
no longer the same hope that they would be
realized at once, and hence no longer the heart to
subordinate everything else to their realization:
I began again to stay up late, having no longer, to
oblige me to go to bed early one evening, the certain
hope of seeing my work begun next morning. I
needed, before I could recover my creative energy, a
few days of relaxation, and the only time my grandmother ventured, in a gentle and disillusioned tone,
to frame the reproach: "Well, this famous work,
don't we even speak about it any more?", I resented
her intrusion, convinced that in her inability to
see that my decision was irrevocably made, she
had further and perhaps for a long time postponed
its execution by the shock which her denial of
justice had administered to my nerves and under
the impact of which I should be disinclined to
begin my work. She felt that her skepticism had
stumbled blindly against a genuine intention.
She apologized, kissing me: "I'm sorry, I shan't
say another word," and, so that I should not be
discouraged, assured me that as soon as I was
quite well again, the work would come of its own
accord to boot. (2: 210–12)

Needless to say, this maternal grandmother—Bathilde Amédée—should have been less "gentle" at the time. But unlike Proust's mother, upon whom the character is based, unlike Monie for that matter, Bathilde never behaved otherwise. (See Tadié 465: "Crippled with grief, [Proust was] only able to write about his mother once he had transformed her into a grandmother, and thus into a fictional character.") She never shamed the narrator. All she ever did, unlike Ya Ya, was set an example—which in her case is nothing to sneeze at.

Shame, according to psychologist Silvan Tomkins, is an "affect," not an emotion—something more natural than cultural, more physical than mental. (Other disciplines define *affect* differently.) That's why we blush, or rather are born able to. (Utter shamelessness must be learned; selfishness, unlearned.) Other such affects are interest, enjoyment, surprise, distress, fear, anger, disgust, and "dissmell," or reaction to stench. For Tomkins, interest and enjoyment are positive, surprise is neutral, and the rest, including shame, are negative. As Elspeth Probyn argues, however, shame can be either negative or positive. It can be used abusively, to humiliate—an attribute of which Sedaris is well aware. Gay-bashers, for example, use shame to manage something as innocuous as homosexuality. It can also be used to nurture, by which I mean to manage truly bad behavior—like gay-bashing. This, too, is an attribute of which Sedaris is well aware—by which I don't just mean that rug.

As both Tomkins and Probyn argue, shame requires interest—an "affective investment" in others. When that investment is questioned and interest interrupted, "we feel deprived."

Crucially, that's when we feel shame. That little moment of disappointment—"oh, but I was

interested"—is amplified into shame or a deep
disappointment in ourselves. Shame marks the
break in connection. We have to care about
something or someone to feel ashamed when
that care and connection—our interest—is not
reciprocated.

Shame, in other words, "illuminates our intense attachment to the world, our desire to be connected with others,
and the knowledge that, as merely human, we will sometimes fail in our attempts to maintain those connections"
(Probyn 13–14). Sedaris, unfortunately, was more interested in the woman's status than in Monie herself—with
whom, in fact, he'd also little contact. That's why their
story—his essay—begins with the obsessive, fetishistic,
self-critical, and almost Proustian paragraph:

> My mother had a great-aunt who lived outside
> of Cleveland and visited us once in Binghamton,
> New York. I was six years old but can clearly
> remember her car moving up the newly paved
> driveway. It was a silver Cadillac driven by a man
> in a flattopped cap, the kind worn by policemen.
> He opened the back door with great ceremony, as
> if this were a coach, and we caught sight of the
> great-aunt's shoes, which were orthopedic yet fancy,
> elaborately tooled leather with little heels the size
> of spools. The shoes were followed by the hem of a
> mink coat, the tip of a cane, and then, finally, the
> great-aunt herself, who was great because she was
> rich and childless. ("Monie Changes Everything" 54)

Marcel at about that age, to his credit, was somewhat
disenchanted by a first glimpse, in church, of the real aris-
tocrat in relation to whom he'd a similar interest: the
Duchesse de Guermantes. "Suddenly, during the nuptial

mass, the verger, by moving to one side, enabled me to see in one of the chapels a fair-haired lady with a large nose, piercing blue eyes, a billowy scarf of mauve silk, glossy and new and bright, and a little pimple at the corner of her nose" (1: 245). (La Rochefoucauld: "Great names debase rather than exalt those who cannot live up to them" [94].) By about sixteen, however, he too was obsessed:

> I was genuinely in love with Mme de Guermantes. The greatest happiness that I could have asked of God would have been that he should send down on her every imaginable calamity, and that ruined, despised, stripped of all the privileges that separated her from me, having no longer any home of her own or people who would condescend to speak to her, she should come to me for asylum. I imagined her doing so. And indeed on those evenings when some change in the atmosphere or in my own state of health brought to the surface of my consciousness some forgotten scroll on which were recorded impressions of other days, instead of profiting by the forces of renewal that had been generated in me, instead of using them to unravel in my own mind thoughts which as a rule escaped me, instead of setting myself at last to work, I preferred to relate aloud, to excogitate in a lively, external manner, with a flow of invention as useless as was my declamation of it, a whole novel crammed with adventure, in which the Duchess, fallen upon misfortune, came to implore assistance from me—who had become, by a converse change of circumstances, rich and powerful. And when I had thus spent hours on end imagining the circumstances, rehearsing the sentences with which I should welcome the Duchess beneath my roof, the

situation remained unaltered; I had, alas, in reality, chosen to love the woman who in her own person combined perhaps the greatest number of different advantages; in whose eyes, accordingly, I could not hope to cut any sort of figure; for she was as rich as the richest commoner—and noble also; not to mention that personal charm which set her at the pinnacle of fashion, made her among the rest a sort of queen. (3: 82–83)

By *love,* of course, Proust doesn't mean anything like what Marcel feels for either his mother or grandmother. He does mean, the man's a snob.

Lou

The father uses shame abusively, as a weapon. His deployments are public, sarcastic, aggressive, sometimes hateful. Like cynical satire, they wound, punish, and destroy. (Like sanguine satire, nurturing shame would cure.) They may target strangers in a restaurant:

> Having arrived at the restaurant of his choice, he lowered his glasses to examine the menu board. "What can you tell me about your boneless Pick O' the Chix combination platter?" he asked the counter girl, a Cherokee teenager wearing a burnt orange synthetic jumper.
>
> "Well, sir, there isn't much *to* say except that it doesn't got any bones and comes with fries and a half-gallon 'Thirsty Man' soda."
>
> My father shouted as if her dusky complexion had somehow affected her hearing. "But the chicken itself, how is it prepared?"

"I put it on a tray," the girl said.

"Oh, I see," my father said. "That explains it all. Golly, you're a bright one, aren't you? IQ just zooming right off the charts. You put it on a tray, do you? I guess that means the chicken is in no position to put itself on the tray, which tells me that it's probably been killed in some fashion. Am I correct? All right, now we're getting somewhere." This continued until the girl was in tears. ("Ashes" 246–47)

They may target his own girls:

My father has always placed a great deal of importance on his daughters' physical beauty. It is, to him, their greatest asset, and he monitors their appearance with the intensity of a pimp. What can I say? He was born a long time ago and is convinced that marriage is a woman's only real shot at happiness. Because it was always assumed that we would lead professional lives, my brother and I were free to grow as plump and ugly as we liked. Our bodies were viewed as mere vehicles, pasty, potbellied machines designed to transport our thoughts from one place to another. I might wander freely through the house drinking pancake batter from a plastic bucket, but the moment one of my sisters overspilled her bikini, my father was right there to mix his metaphors. "Jesus, Flossie, what are we running here, a dairy farm? Look at you, you're the size of a house. Two more pounds, and you won't be able to cross state lines without a trucking license."

"He honestly thought he was doing his girls a favor," Sedaris explains, "and it confused him when the thanks never came" ("A Shiner Like a Diamond" 133).

More to the point, the deployments target Sedaris. A relatively benign instance occurred whenever he, Sedaris, did something truly stupid:

> As a child I'd always harbored a sneaking
> suspicion that I might be a genius. The theory was
> completely my own, corroborated by no one, but so
> what? Being misunderstood was all part of the
> package. My father occasionally referred to me as
> "Smart Guy," but eventually I realized that when
> saying it, he usually meant the opposite.
> "Hey, Smart Guy—coating your face with
> mayonnaise because you can't find the insect
> repellent."
> "Hey, Smart Guy, thinking you can toast
> marshmallows in your bedroom."
> That type of thing. ("Smart Guy" 241)

A malign one occurred when, after dropping out of college for the second time and then traveling across the country, Sedaris found himself back in North Carolina and living with his parents. Loafing, really. After six months spent waking at noon, getting high, and listening to the same Joni Mitchell record over and over again, he was called into Lou's den and, not surprisingly, told to get out. "I felt as though he were firing me from the job of being his son," Sedaris recalls. Surprisingly, this eviction—this termination, in effect—had nothing to do with laziness:

> I wouldn't know it until months later, but my
> father had kicked me out of the house not because
> I was a bum but because I was gay. Our little talk
> was supposed to be one of those defining moments
> that shape a person's adult life, but he'd been so
> uncomfortable with the most important word that
> he'd left it out completely, saying only, "I think we

both know why I'm doing this." I guess I could have pinned him down, I just hadn't seen the point. "Is it because I'm a failure? A drug addict? A sponge? Come on, Dad, just give me one good reason."

"Who wants to say that?" he explains. As far as we know, Lou never apologized. Sharon did at the time, more or less for him. "She cried until it sounded as if she were choking. 'I'm sorry,' she said. 'I'm sorry, I'm sorry, I'm sorry'" ("Hejira" 87–89). Sedaris, nowadays, more or less forgives.

But what can *I* say? The man's a homophobe. Too homophobic, at any rate, to have parented a gay child. He's selfish, too—if not lazy. Too selfish, at any rate, to parent almost anyone. Lou would promise to pick up the kids but then stay home watching television. They'd hitchhike. (See "Planet of the Apes" 121–23.) He'd promise them ice cream but then go to a golf tournament. They'd hate it. (See "The Women's Open" 53–55.) He'd promise a beach house but then get something only he wanted:

> By our final day of vacation our father had decided that instead of building a place on Emerald Island, we should improve the home we already had. "Maybe add a pool," he said. "What do you kids think about that?" Nobody answered.
>
> By the time he'd finished wheedling it down, the house at the beach had become a bar in the basement.

In fact, the man's too selfish to have married anyone. Whereas having to care for that mother-in-law—which should have been Lou's responsibility—was the last thing Sharon needed, she did need that house. And so in the years to come, as if carried by the tide, "our mother drifted farther and farther away, first to twin beds and then down the hall to a room decorated with seascapes and baskets of sun-bleached sand dollars" ("The Ship Shape" 27–29).

Marcel's father, in *Remembrance of Things Past,* is almost unheard of. One character, though, can be almost paternally cruel: the Baron de Charlus. Charlus is the Duchesse de Guermantes's brother-in-law. He's also a closet case. One night, in their seaside hotel, Charlus makes a sexual advance that Marcel—still sixteen—fails to detect. The next morning, on the beach at "Balbec," Charlus tells Marcel that Bathilde is waiting for him. "I was [then] greatly surprised to hear him say, pinching my neck as he spoke with a familiarity and a laugh that were frankly vulgar: 'But he doesn't care a fig for his old grandmother, does he, eh? Little rascal!'" Not knowing this was a bit of a tease, let alone another advance, Marcel responds: "What, Monsieur! I adore her!" (2: 473). To this, in what's remembered as a "torrent of abuse" (3: 760), Charlus him-self responds:

> "Monsieur . . . you are still young; you should profit by your youth to learn two things: first, to refrain from expressing sentiments that are too natural not to be taken for granted; and secondly not to rush into speech in reply to things that are said to you before you have penetrated their meaning. If you had taken this precaution a moment ago you would have saved yourself the appearance of speaking at cross-purposes like a deaf man, thereby adding a second absurdity to that of having anchors embroidered on your bathing dress."

"You make me realize that I was premature in speak-ing to you last night of the charms of youth," the speech concludes. "I should have done you a greater service had

I pointed out to you its thoughtlessness, its inconse-
quence, and its want of comprehension" (2: 473–74). There
were other such torrents to come. There was forgiveness
as well.

Sedaris, to his credit, can be as self-deprecatory in
fiction about fathers as in the nonfiction mentioned above.
One narrator, an unnamed fourteen-year-old, complains
about having been given "a set of golf clubs that, my father
likes to remind me, cost a goddamned fortune."

> He says that he would give his right arm for such a
> beautiful set of clubs. The obvious solution would be
> for him to take the stinking clubs and give me what
> I wanted in the first place. ("My Manuscript" 23)

What he'd wanted, admirably enough, was a typewriter.
But what he needs one for is such ludicrous pornography as:

> "Oh, Chad," Mrs. Holt called brightly in her
> irritating and bright voice. "There's someone here to
> see you!"
> Chad groaned and stepped out of the shower,
> taking special care to dry his ~~four inch his seven
> inch his~~ enormous thirteen-and-a-half-inch ~~penis~~
> cock. He was a stud—*and he knew it.* His ass was
> still a little sore from last night's marathon drill
> sesh with the guys at the auto plant, but other
> than that he had no complaints. Wearing only a
> scant towel, he stepped into the kitchen, where he
> received a gigantic shock at the sight of his ~~hideous
> nosy hateful~~ family surrounded by a dozen naked
> but heavily armed ~~guys~~ studs.

"Chad Holt," he needlessly remarks, "is my name in the
book" (22, 28, emphasis and redaction original). Of course
what it really is may be David Sedaris.

The fiction, however, doesn't forgive. It's even rather mean—much like father stories by Franz Kafka (1883–1924). (See, for example, "The Judgment" [1913] and "The Metamorphosis" [1915].) In one Sedaris story, a selfish, status-conscious father donates twin boys to some homeless sex offender in order to beat an equally "generous" competitor. Such generosity, the father reports, "can induce feelings of shame, inadequacy, and even envy."

> Why needlessly escalate when we all knew what was most important? After a brief conference, Beth and I called the tramp back over and asked which he liked better, young boys or young girls. Much to our delight he said that girls were too much of a headache but that he'd had some fun with boys before his last visit to our local state penitentiary. That said, we gave him our ten-year-old sons, Taylor and Weston. Top that, Neighbor! ("Christmas Means Giving" 128, 130)

The boys, of course, are murdered. The father himself ends up homeless.

In another, more disturbing story—more disturbing because less fantastic—a twelve-year-old named Chug imagines watching his physically abusive "asshole" of a father have to beg some record executive for a contract. To keep from laughing at this "pathetic display," he reports, "I will have to bite the inside of my cheeks."

> Blood will rise up in my throat—that same bitter taste you get after absentmindedly holding a coat hanger in your mouth.

The father throws Chug out of the house. The boy himself ends up abusive. Inadvertently called "dipshit" by nephew Marty, "I took the meat of his thigh and twisted it between my fingers." Marty having accidentally pulled his hair, "I popped him across the face" ("Jamboree," 98, 109, 110).

It's easy to see from whom Sedaris learned both to be selfish and to use shame abusively. Yet, as hinted above ("too selfish to parent *almost* anyone"), Lou did nurture his other son—whom he'd never call Smart Guy and who, for some reason, calls himself "the Rooster":

> Unlike the rest of us, the Rooster has always enjoyed our father's support and encouragement. With the dream of college officially dead and buried, he sent my brother to technical school, hoping he might develop an interest in computers. Three weeks into the semester, Paul dropped out, and my father, convinced that his son's lawn-mowing skills bordered on genius, set him up in the landscaping business. "I've seen him in action, and what he does is establish a pattern and really tackle it!"
>
> Eventually, my brother fell into the floor-sanding business. It's hard work, but he enjoys the satisfaction that comes with a well-finished rec room. He thoughtfully called his company Silly P's Hardwood Floors, Silly P being the name he would have chosen were he a rap star. When my father suggested that the word *silly* might frighten away some of the upper-tier customers, Paul considered changing the name to Silly Fucking P's Hardwood Floors. The work puts him in contact with plumbers and carpenters from such towns as Bunn and Clayton, men who offer dating advice such as "If she's old enough to bleed, she's old enough to breed."
>
> "Old enough to what?" my father asks. "Oh, Paul, those aren't the sort of people you need to be

associating with. What are you doing with hayseeds like that? The goal is to better yourself. Meet some intellectuals. Read a book!"

Not for nothing, Paul is straight. What more can I say—other than that, to his own credit, Lou's nurtured in return:

> After all these years our father has never understood that we, his children, tend to gravitate toward the very people he's spent his life warning us about. Most of us have left town, but my brother remains in Raleigh. He was there when our mother died and still, years later, continues to help our father grieve: "The past is gone, hoss. What you need now is some motherfucking pussy." While my sisters and I offer sympathy long-distance, Paul is the one who arrives at our father's house on Thanksgiving day, offering to prepare traditional Greek dishes to the best of his ability. It is a fact that he once made a tray of spanakopita using Pam rather than melted butter. Still, though, at least he tries. ("You Can't Kill the Rooster" 66–67)

Sharon

The mother was lazy. She never worked. She never cleaned. Her "hobbies," to hear Sedaris tell it, were smoking, sleeping, and Sidney Sheldon ("Genetic Engineering" 33). That, and television. Here he is—irritated—at ten:

> While my mother was pregnant with her sixth child, my father finally gave in and allowed her to hire a housekeeper one day a week. When Lena was introduced I thought that finally we were getting somewhere. I left for school as my mother turned on the portable TV and handed her a cup of coffee. I returned from school seven hours later to find an ironing board in the kitchen, Mom and Lena in roughly the same position—watching TV and drinking coffee.

Struck by their perfect union—"the two laziest people on the face of the earth" coming together to watch *General*

Hospital—Sedaris ran to the vacuum cleaner. It was cold ("The Curly Kind" 162).

Sedaris, thereafter, tried everything. Even shame. Here he is in ninth grade, about to act in *Hamlet:*

> "Perchance, fair lady, thou dost think me unduly vexed by the sorrowful state of thine quarters," I said to my mother as I ran the vacuum cleaner over the living-room carpet she was inherently too lazy to bother with. "These foul specks, the evidence of life itself, have sullied not only thine shag-tempered mat but also thine character. Be ye mad, woman? Were it a punishable crime to neglect thine dwellings, you, my feeble-spirited mistress, would hang from the tallest tree in penitence for your shameful ways. See ye not the porcelain plates and hearty mugs waiting to be washed clean of evidence? Get thee to thine work, damnable lady, and quickly, before the products of thine very loins raise their collected fists in a spirit born both of rage and indignation, forcibly coaxing the last breath from the foul chamber of thine vain and upright throat. Go now, wastrel, and get to it!"

Such shame, however, never did the trick. In this case, Sharon reacted as if whipped "with a short length of yarn."

> The intent was there, but the weapon was strange and inadequate. I could tell by the state of my room that she spent the next day searching my dresser for drugs. The clothes I took pride in neatly folding were crammed tight into their drawers with no regard for color or category. ("The Drama Bug" 97)

It was the mess that bothered Sedaris at the time, not the sloth. He himself was just as lazy. So were his siblings. It's easy, of course, to see from whom they learned it:

During the first week of September, it was
my family's habit to rent a beach house on Ocean
Isle, a thin strip of land off the coast of North
Carolina. As youngsters, we participated in all
the usual seaside activities—which were fun,
until my father got involved and systematically
chipped away at our pleasure. Miniature golf
was ruined with a lengthy dissertation on
impact, trajectory, and wind velocity, and our
sand castles were critiqued with stifling lectures
on the dynamics of the vaulted ceiling. We
enjoyed swimming, until the mystery of the tides
was explained in such a way that the ocean
seemed nothing more than an enormous
saltwater toilet, flushing itself on a sad and
predictable basis.

By the time we reached our teens, we were
exhausted. No longer interested in the water, we
joined our mother on the beach blanket and
dedicated ourselves to the higher art of tanning.
Under her guidance, we learned which lotions to
start off with, and what worked best for various
weather conditions and times of day. She taught
us that the combination of false confidence and
Hawaiian Tropic could result in a painful and
unsightly burn, certain to subtract valuable
points when, on the final night of vacation,
contestants gathered for the Miss Emollient
Pageant. This was a contest judged by our mother,
in which the holder of the darkest tan was
awarded a crown, a sash, and a scepter. ("Genetic
Engineering" 34–35)

Nowadays, it's having complained that bothers Sedaris.
It was his behavior, not hers, that's shameful.

Sloth, of course, wasn't all they learned from Sharon. According to Sedaris, however, it's the only vice. The drinking, he feels, was something else—possibly another hobby. The insults were both justified and funny. Here's Sharon, somewhat abusive, on both Lou and Ya Ya, but on herself as well:

> "Tell that cow of yours to tone it down a little," my mother would shout from her stool in the breakfast nook. "They can hear her chewing her cud all the way to the state line."
>
> "Oh, Sharon," my father would sigh.
>
> "Oh, Sharon, my fat ass," my mother would shout. Moments later she would rethink her exact wording, adding, "It's fat, my ass, but not as big as the can on that prize heifer you've got shoveling down three sacks of clover she harvested from the Kazmerzacks' front yard, mama's boy." ("Get Your Ya-Ya's Out!" 31–32)

The aversion to sentiment—nearly Modernist—stemmed from knowing what it masks. (I'm thinking of both Lytton Strachey and Virginia Woolf.) One night, Sedaris ended a phone call to Sharon with *I love you:*

> "I'm going to pretend I didn't hear that," she said. I heard a match strike in the background, the tinkling of ice cubes in a raised glass. And then she hung up. I had never said such a thing to my mother, and if I had it to do over again, I would probably take it back. Nobody ever spoke that way except Lisa. It was queer to say such a thing to someone unless you were either trying to talk them out of money or into bed, our mother had taught that when we were no taller than pony kegs. I had known people who said such things to their

parents, "I love you," but it always translated to mean, "I'd love to get off the phone with you." ("Ashes" 240)

The aversion here may also stem from Sharon's having known that *I love you* is a demand she couldn't satisfy. It's a demand for the impossible reply: *I love you, too,* said simultaneously. (See Barthes, *A Lover's Discourse* 102.) Sedaris, incidentally, is the child to have emerged both next best smoker and next best drinker after Sharon, not to mention drug addict. (La Rochefoucauld: "Nothing is so contagious as an example, and our every really good or bad action inspires a similar one. We imitate good deeds through emulation and evil ones because of the evil of our nature which, having been held in check by shame, is now set free by example" [230].) Paul emerged next most insulting. Paul, again, least maudlin.

If the smoking, the drinking, the insults, and the aversion to sentiment aren't vices, for Sedaris, nor are they virtues. Sharon, however, was basically good. She was both instinctively egalitarian and willfully benevolent. The egalitarianism is perhaps best exemplified by Sedaris coming home to find Sharon and Lena in "roughly the same" physical position. For Sharon, they're in the same metaphysical one. It's also exemplified by Lisa, to almost everyone's surprise, coming home for the holidays with some prostitute. Sharon alone treats the woman as a guest:

> "Mom, this is Dinah. Dinah, this is my mother."
>
> "Oh, thank goodness," my mother said, helping our guest out of her shoddy rabbit jacket. "For a moment there, I was afraid you were one of those damned carolers. I wasn't expecting company, so you'll have to excuse the way I look."

"The way *she* looked?" thought Sedaris. Dinah's mascara had smeared, causing her to resemble a "ridiculously costumed panda," and here his *mother* was apologizing?

> "Whore," I whispered. "That lady is a whore." I'm not sure what reaction I was after, but shock would have done quite nicely. Instead, my mother said, "Well, then, we should probably offer her a drink." ("Dinah, the Christmas Whore" 117, emphasis original)

The benevolence is best exemplified in Sedaris's fiction. One father—he's the narrator, as in "Christmas Means Giving"—performs surgery on his own child because, like Lou, the man's both selfish and cheap. Unfortunately, he's incompetent:

> I am not a physician but have read enough to know that everything is not as complicated as it is made to sound. Most of it is just common sense. For example, I have given my daughter, Dawn, stitches several times. If you can sew a button on a shirt, then you can give someone stitches. Just make sure to use a clean, sharp needle and some strong thread. I recommend unwaxed dental floss. Do not, under any circumstances, use yarn. I found myself in a pinch last year and Dawn still blames me for that scar on her forehead. I said then and I will say now that there is no way I'm going to pay some doctor three hundred dollars. ("Music for Lovers" 13)

One mother—fortunately competent—does so because she'd no alternative:

> One year ago on a frosty Christmas morning, a young widowed mother, poor as dirt but still

attractive in her own way, took drastic measures
to save the life of a five-year-old child who was
dying of kidney failure. She had no health
insurance or dialysis machine but she did have a
heavy Bible which she used to whack the boy
against the back of the head, knocking him out in
order to spare him the pain that would follow.
Taking a rusty penknife and a simple, dime-store
sewing kit, the young woman proceeded to remove
one of her kidneys and successfully transplant the
vital organ into her son's vulnerable body. ("Based
Upon a True Story" 111)

Although he doesn't know it, this narrator's both sentimental and sanctimonious. Nor did that father know he's
cheap. Whereas Sedaris, in the nonfiction, ridicules himself on purpose, all such narrators, in the fiction, do so by
accident. Sedaris, as the primary target of his autobiographical satire, is now self-conscious. These other people—
also targets—are not. Even—or especially—the alter egos.

Like Monie with the rug, Sharon used shame to nurture. Unlike Lou, that is, she used shame to make children
realize both how foolish or vicious they were and that they
could do something about it. In particular, she made them
realize how selfish or snobbish they were, how nonbenevo-
lent or nonegalitarian. Such fostering of self-consciousness
required the suspension—for the right amount of time—
of what Tomkins calls "interest," Probyn calls "affective
investment," and Sedaris *attention*. Clearly though, in
Sharon's case, they all mean love—or rather, the kind of
love she didn't verbalize:

"Of course you love Ya Ya," [Lou] would say.
"She's your grandmother." He stated it as a natural
consequence, when to our mind, that was hardly
the case. Someone might be your blood relative, but

it didn't mean you had to love her. Our magazine articles and afternoon talk shows were teaching us that people had to earn their love from one day to the next. My father's family relied on a set of rules that no longer applied. It wasn't enough to provide your children with a home and hand over all your loose change, a person had to be *fun* while doing it. For Ya Ya it was too late, but there was still time for my father, who over the next few years grew increasingly nervous. He observed my mother holding court in the bedroom and wondered how she did it. She might occasionally snap, but once the smoke cleared we were back at her feet, fighting for her attention. ("Get Your Ya-Ya's Out!" 37, emphasis original)

Maternal love, that is. Other kinds, Sharon did verbalize—if, that is, "flushed with wine [and] pounding the tabletop." *Love?* she'd ask in such condition. "'I love a good steak cooked rare. I love my cat, and I love . . .' My sisters and I leaned forward, waiting to hear our names. 'Tums,' our mother said. 'I love Tums'" ("Me Talk Pretty One Day" 169).

"You're a snob," she snapped—in private—one time Sedaris pretended being rich. "That's your problem in a hard little nutshell. I grew up around people like you, and you know what? I couldn't stand them. Nobody could" ("Chipped Beef" 4). That, for some reason, seems to have done the trick right away. Often, though, more time was needed. When Sedaris humiliated Lena about being poor and having to raise poultry, Sharon "tried in vain to convey the shame I had brought against her." ("I don't need your filthy chickens," Sedaris had told the housekeeper in front of her children. "We buy our own—from the store.") He simply wasn't listening. His only response was to swear off chicken for the next few weeks. And it was years before Sedaris "thought of things differently" ("The Curly Kind" 163).

Bathilde too, in *Remembrance of Things Past,* managed to undo Marcel's "snobbery" over time—though not through belated shame. (Proust, in fact, does use the English word.) She'd simply set an egalitarian example. Marcel, in mourning her death, grows to resemble her this way—a development of which he's completely unaware. Freud calls this *introjection.* Without knowing it, that is, Marcel becomes less and less interested in aristocracy. (See Goodkin 131–44.) Proust knew it, of course—even though, in mourning his mother's death, he himself seems to have done no such thing.

One instance of shaming Sedaris out of selfishness— also in private, also successful at the time—involved the death of Ya Ya, plus false grief:

> I was in my second year of college when I received the news that Ya Ya had died. My mother called to tell me. I cradled the phone beneath my chin, a joint in one hand and a beer in the other, and noticed the time, 11:22 A.M. My roommate was listening in, and because I wanted to impress him as a sensitive and complex individual, I threw myself onto the bed and made the most of my grief. "It can't be true," I cried. "It can't be true-hu-hu-hu-hu." My sobs sounded as if I were reading them off a page. "A-ha-ha-ha-ha-ha. A-hu-hu-haw-haw-haw-haw-haw." I had just finished reading Truman Capote's *A Christmas Memory* and tried to pass it off as my own. "I feel like a piece of my soul has been ripped away and now I'm just a kite," I said rubbing my eyes in an effort to provoke tears.

"I'll walk across the campus later this afternoon and search the sky, expecting to find two clouds shaped like hearts."

"I've got just the thing for you, bud," my roommate said. ("Get Your Ya-Ya's Out!" 37–38)

His remedy involved two hits of acid, a bag of ice cubes, and a needle. So they split the hits, then a pair of posts, and sat hallucinating in the dormitory kitchen as some criminal-justice major pierced their ears.

Sedaris flew home the next day. "There's no way you're coming into my house with an earring," Lou said. "No sir, no way." So Sedaris spent the next few hours in the carport, threatening to sleep in the station wagon, unwilling to compromise himself. "Asshole!" he yelled. "Nazi!"

"Listen," my mother said, stepping out the door with a tray of marble-sized meatballs. "You take the earring out, we go to the funeral, you stick it back in before you catch your plane. The hole won't close up that quickly, take my word for it. This is something I want you to do for your father, all right?" She set the tray upon the hood of the car and picked up a meatball, studying it for a moment. "Besides that, an earring looks really stupid combined with glasses. It sends a mixed message, and the effect is, well, it's troubling. Give me the earring and I'll put it away for you. Then I want you to come inside and help me straighten up the house. The Greeks will be here tomorrow afternoon, and we need to hide the booze."

Sedaris removed the earring and never put it back. "Looking back," he writes, "it shames me that I chose that particular moment to make a stand" ("Get Your Ya-Ya's Out!" 38–39).

Another such instance occurred about ten years earlier. Relatively new, oddball neighbors from whom Sedaris
had been keeping his distance yet about whom he was
inordinately curious showed up in costume on the night
after Halloween. Sharon, out of candy, signaled Sedaris to
get them some of his own. Although allergic to chocolate,
he'd rather not:

I knew that it was just a matter of time before
she came into my room and started collecting the
candy herself, grabbing indiscriminately with no
regard to my rating system. Had I been thinking
straight, I would have hidden the most valuable
items in my dresser drawer, but instead, panicked
by the thought of her hand on my doorknob, I tore
off the wrappers and began cramming the candy
bars into my mouth, desperately, like someone in a
contest. Most were miniature, which made them
easier to accommodate, but still there was only so
much room, and it was hard to chew and fit more in
at the same time. The headache began immediately,
and I chalked it up to tension.

My mother told the Tomkeys she needed to
check on something, and then she opened the door
and stuck her head inside my room. "What the *hell*
are you doing?" she whispered, but my mouth was
too full to answer. "I'll just be a moment," she
called, and as she closed the door behind her and
moved toward my bed, I began breaking the wax
lips and candy necklaces pulled from pile no. 2.
These were the second-best things I had received,
and while it hurt to destroy them, it would have
hurt even more to give them away. I had just
started to mutilate a miniature box of Red Hots
when my mother pried them from my hands,

accidentally finishing the job for me. BB-size pellets clattered onto the floor, and as I followed them with my eyes, she snatched up a roll of Necco wafers.

"Not those," I pleaded, but rather than words, my mouth expelled chocolate, chewed chocolate, which fell onto the sleeve of her sweater. "Not those. Not those."

She shook her arm, and the mound of chocolate dropped like a horrible turd upon my bedspread. "You should look at yourself," she said. "I mean, *really* look at yourself."

Along with the Necco wafers she took several Tootsie Pops and half a dozen caramels wrapped in cellophane. I heard her apologize to the Tomkeys for her absence, and then I heard my candy hitting the bottom of their bags.

Sedaris had protected and watched over these people for months, he reflects, but now, with one stupid act, they'd turned his "pity" into something ugly:

The shift wasn't gradual, but immediate, and it provoked an uncomfortable feeling of loss. We hadn't been friends, the Tomkeys and I, but still I had given them the gift of my curiosity. Wondering about the Tomkey family had made me feel generous, but now I would have to shift gears and find pleasure in hating them. The only alternative was to do as my mother had instructed and take a good look at myself. This was an old trick, designed to turn one's hatred inward, and while I was determined not to fall for it, it was hard to shake the mental picture snapped by her suggestion: here is a boy sitting on a bed, his mouth smeared with chocolate. He's a human being, but also he's a pig, surrounded by trash and gorging himself so

that others may be denied. ("Us and Them" 10–11,
12, emphasis original)

In other words, Sharon was a good parent to all six
kids; Lou, to Paul alone. It was she who truly nurtured
them. But she wasn't perfect. Forcing Sedaris to relinquish candy, for example, and *as* an example, was really
pretty bad. Why not suggest he do so? Why not ask him to?
Why not tell the truth? *I'm sorry, we're out of candy.* After
all, she'd never let *him* get away with such a thing. When,
at thirteen, Sedaris gave a beggar some of Sharon's money
without permission, she made him retrieve it. "If you want
to give her a dollar, that's your own business," she said.
"But that dollar was mine" ("The Change in Me" 73). Forcing them, as children, to parent her—if only on occasion—
was also bad. It's not like Paul's having chosen, as an
adult, to nurture Lou. But Sharon couldn't help it. They
knew she couldn't. And so they forgave her, even at the
time. A few years before the beggar incident, heavy snow
kept them home from school for a week. Sharon, understandably, had a little breakdown—not so much nervous,
perhaps, as alcoholic. "Normally she waited until five
o'clock to have a drink, but for the past few days she'd been
making an exception. Drinking didn't count if you followed a glass of wine with a cup of coffee." She threw them
out of the house, then locked the door. It wasn't until several hours later that another neighbor made her take them
in. "[W]e saw our mother," Sedaris recalls, "this puffy figure awkwardly negotiating the crest of the hill. She did not
own a pair of pants, and her legs were buried to the calves
in snow. We wanted to send her home, to kick her out of
nature just as she had kicked us out of the house, but it
was hard to stay angry at someone that pitiful-looking."

"Are you wearing your *loafers?*" Lisa asked,
and in response, our mother raised her bare foot.

"I *was* wearing loafers," she said. "I mean, really, it was there a second ago."

This was how things went. One moment she was locking us out of our own house and the next we were rooting around in the snow, looking for her left shoe. "Oh, forget about it," she said. "It'll turn up in a few days." Gretchen fitted her cap over my mother's foot. Lisa secured it with her scarf, and surrounding her tightly on all sides, we made our way back home. ("Let It Snow" 14, 16, emphasis original)

The feeling of pity, like the feeling of love, is an emotion, not an affect—something more cultural than natural, more mental than physical. Of course, they're a lot alike.

Sharon's weakness as a parent is also best exemplified in Sedaris's fiction. One mother—on the one hand—was just plain "mean" ("Barrel Fever" 137). She'd kept a file marked "POISON" containing terrible, unsent messages to her children: son Adolph Heck the narrator (named after Hitler), and daughters Faith, Hope, Joy, and Charity. (Like Proust, who omits brother Robert in *Remembrance of Things Past,* Sedaris, here, omits any transformation of Paul. Like Paul, Robert was straight. Like Paul, he was younger. Unlike Paul, he was the only sibling. Critics call such omissions *paralipsis* [see Genette 51].) All five of them, shortly after her death, rummage through this file. "How could she possibly be so cruel?" the girls ask:

"I am not the 'missing link,' I am not, I am *not,"* Joy chanted, holding a draft of her graduation card. "I am *not* 'God's gift to fraternity beer baths,' I am not, I am not, I am not." Charity and Faith gathered round and the three of them embraced in a circle of healing. There were letters to me, comparing me

unfavorably to both Richard Speck and the late
Stepin Fetchit, but in all honesty it really didn't
bother me too much. We all entertain hateful
thoughts every now and then. ("Barrel Fever" 128,
emphasis original)

On the other hand, she was benevolent. Every single one
of fifteen years' worth of New Year's resolutions, also filed,
turn out to read: *Be good.* Adolph's, oddly enough, say the
same.

Another mother tells the daughter who comes to her
in search of love and understanding: "If you're looking for
sympathy you can find it between shit and syphilis in the
dictionary" ("The Last You'll Hear from Me" 20). But the
girl—the narrator—deserves it. She herself is mean beyond
belief, probably beyond ever doing something about it.

Marty's mother, in "Jamboree," is terribly negligent.
But according to Chug, the boy was repulsive.

Don Singleton, a narrator with the same initials as
Sedaris as well as nearly the same life, imagines having made a film in which "insult comedian" Don Rickles
played his mother. But Rickles's insults, unlike what
we're told of Sharon's, are both unjustified and lame. *You
hockey puck,* for example, is the man's signature. They're
more abusive as well, not to mention never self-directed.
And given both the coincidence of their first names and
the fact that it's really Singleton, not Singleton's mother,
who's both insulting and abusive, the comedian should
have been him:

In my movie, *Don's Story,* my parents are played
by Charles Bronson and Don Rickles. I think they
both did a fantastic job—especially Don Rickles,
who played the part of my mother. Quite a few
actresses were eager for that role, but as director
I chose Don Rickles not because my mother is

funny—far from it—and not to boost Mr. Rickles's career, but because, ha ha, you put a wig on that guy and he looks just exactly like her. Ha Ha. ("Don's Story" 72)

Sharon's death—from lung cancer—traumatized all her children. Paul finds consolation, to some extent, in having had children of his own and Lou to himself. (See "Baby Einstein" 231–45.) Sedaris finds consolation in writing. Amy finds it in both writing and acting. Where Lisa, Gretchen, and Tiffany find it, I couldn't say. Sometimes Sedaris's writing addresses that death directly, autobiographically—as in "Ashes." Sometimes it does so indirectly—in fiction like "Barrel Fever." All the writing, however, or at least most of it, may be addressed—primarily—to Sharon herself. As such, it's meant in part to revive her. This would be true regardless of the writer's sexuality as well as of the kind of relationship involved: parent-child, as here; teacher-student; and so on. Given his sexuality, however, the writing by Sedaris—like that of Proust—might also be meant to tell her something. Might *still* be meant to tell her something, rather, as with work done before his mother's death. What, exactly? That he's gay. To quote one critic—Eve Kosofsky Sedgwick—on *Remembrance of Things Past:*

> Is it not the mother to whom both the coming-out testament and its continued refusal to come out are addressed? And isn't some scene like that behind the persistent force of the novel's trope: "the profanation of the mother"? That that woman who lovingly and fearfully scrutinizes narrator and narrative *can't know* is both an analytic inference (she never acts as if she knows, and anyway how could she know?) and a blank imperative: she *mustn't* know. (248, emphasis original)

Other such "testaments," as I'll explore in "André," may include Oscar Wilde's *De Profundis* (1897), André Gide's *The Immoralist* (1921), even Marguerite Yourcenar's *Alexis* (1929). Unlike Proust, however, Sedaris—as an adult—has never "refused" to come out. He's been honest that way. Unlike Proust's mother, moreover, or that of Marcel, or even Bathilde, Sharon wasn't homophobic. (Recall that apology for Lou: "I'm sorry, I'm sorry, I'm sorry" ["Hejira" 89].) Nor was she "fearful." In fact, Sharon resembles a far more American—and far less profanable—figure than any of them: the bitchy—I mean virago-like mother. Think: Ethel Merman as Rose, in the musical *Gypsy* (1959). Or Roseanne Barr as herself. And as writing by the son of a such a—no, not bitch. As writing by the son of this virago, not only do the collections *Barrel Fever, Naked, Holidays on Ice, Me Talk Pretty One Day,* and *Dress Your Family in Corduroy and Denim* both address Sharon and, to a lesser extent, address her death, they also *impersonate* her. And I'm not describing introjection here, or that alone. For one thing, such impersonation is relatively self-conscious. Sedaris, to some extent, knows its happening. For another, the impersonation is also true, once again, of work done before his mother's death.

So the five collections speak both to and *as* Sharon. Why, exactly? Because she'd always encouraged Sedaris to do such a thing. She'd always encouraged him—no, not just to shame. (Recall the similarity of nurturing shame and sanguine satire: both curative.) She'd always encouraged him, once again by setting an example, to perform. To quote another critic—D. A. Miller—on the female stars and starstruck chorus boys of shows like *Gypsy* (others include *Mame* [1966], *Applause* [1970], and *La Cage aux Folles* [1983]):

> [Why should a chorus boy] brave such stigma
> at all if he hadn't been enlisted under the power—

more ancient and tenacious—of a *solicitation?* For if he now finds himself putting up with a theater whose clientele throws fruit at him, it is because his desire to perform was first exercised elsewhere, through a so much more heartening modeling of theatrical identities and relations that, in effect, he still hasn't left this earlier stage, where, just as he had taken his first steps, or uttered his first words there, he would sing and dance for a woman who called him to performance, and acclaimed him with applause even before he was through, prompting him if he faltered with some song or dance of her own, almost as though she were coaching him to be her understudy in a role that either generosity, or timidity, or some other thing kept her from playing herself. (*Place for Us* 80–81, emphasis original)

Or if not some song and dance of *his* own, then some "yarn"-like recitation—some "Drama Bug" *avant la letter*—such as that shameful yet impressive attempt to make Sharon clean her room: "Perchance, fair lady, thou dost think me unduly vexed" ("The Drama Bug" 97). Not that she applauded—at least, not just yet. And not that she had to—yet. Such acclaim, like *I love you,* could usually go without saying.

Sometimes, though, it couldn't. But before I say when, let me also say that not only did Sharon use shame as something other than a weapon, and not only could she be insulting ("Tell that cow of yours to tone it down a little"), she also—unlike Charlus—knew both how and when to tease, but also when not to. By *tease,* I mean that whereas Sharon usually socialized children by putting herself above them, as a parent who'd "snapped," she also, on occasion, did so rather amiably—which is to say, more or less at their level. Here's one example: When Sedaris, stammering "I just want to be friends," rejected what he mistakenly perceived as a sexual advance on her part, Sharon studied him for a minute and then sighed: "Damn, and here you've been leading me on all this time" ("Next of Kin" 44). This too, like the recitation, had been just before the *Hamlet*—with Sedaris in ninth grade, at about fourteen. Here's another example: When Sedaris had a bad time rehearsing *Hamlet*—among other injustices, his role had been reduced to the line: "Aye, my lord"— Sharon teased: "Are we *vexed?*" ("The Drama Bug" 103, emphasis added). This question, by repeating that Elizabethan term, playfully tossed "Perchance, fair lady, thou dost think me unduly vexed" back at Sedaris. But it applauded the recitation as well—figuratively speaking. It acknowledged—acclaimed, even—a verbal skill so very like her own.

Here, then, is an example of Sharon's knowing both when not to tease and when to applaud: "You were the best in the whole show," she told him on opening night. It was just the two of them in the car, after stopping at a grocery store on their way home. She alone of all the family had attended *Hamlet*. "I mean it," she added, "you walked onto that stage and all eyes went right to you." This, however, was one performance even Sedaris knew had sucked, one performance that—unlike the recitation—couldn't possibly have impressed anyone. Not even Sharon. Or rather, *especially* Sharon. And so it occurred to him that she was a better actor than he could ever hope to be.

Acting is different than posing or pretending. When done with precision, it bears a striking resemblance to lying. Stripped of the costumes and grand gestures, it presents itself as an unquestionable truth. I didn't envy my mother's skill, neither did I contradict her. That's how convincing she was. It seemed best, sitting beside her with a frozen pizza thawing on my lap, to simply sit back and learn. ("The Drama Bug" 105)

Henry

Sedaris has troubled relations with all but one sister. He either pities or is annoyed by both older sister Lisa and youngest sister, Tiffany, each of whom, like Sedaris himself, made a "mess" of her life ("Twelve Moments in the Life of the Artist" 57). Chug's sister in "Jamboree"— nephew Marty's mother—fictionalizes the two of them: pitiful, annoying, and negligent. He envies both Tiffany and younger sister Gretchen, with their greater talent for visual art. This superiority on Gretchen's part was first made clear in high school:

> Asked to render a bowl of grapes, I would turn in
> what resembled a pile of stones hovering above
> a whitewall tire. My sister's paintings were
> prominently displayed on the walls of the
> classroom, and the teacher invoked her name
> whenever discussing perspective or color. She was
> included in all the city- and countywide shows and

never mentioned the blue ribbons scotch-taped to
her entries. Had she been a braggart, it would have
been much easier to hate her. As it was, I had to
wrestle daily with both my inadequacy and my
uncontrollable jealousy. I didn't want to kill her,
but hoped someone else might do the job for me.
("Twelve Moments in the Life of the Artist" 41–42)

Despite or possibly because of this experience—this example, really—Sedaris both majored in art, before quitting college, and then went to art school in Chicago.
Sharon, with Monie money, had paid.

Only Amy, another younger sister, is an equal. Like
Sedaris, as mentioned above, she's a writer. In fact, the
two collaborate as "The Talent Family." Like Sedaris,
moreover, she does satire. She's the cocreator of *Strangers
with Candy,* a TV show (1999–2000) and now film (2006)
that target the "after-school special." This unique bond
may stem from Amy's having been the one sister to approximate Sharon as friend—or ami-able teaser (pun intended).
Once, back in art school:

I'd been riding the Chicago el with my sister Amy,
who was getting off three or four stops ahead of me.
The doors opened, and as she stepped out of the
crowded car, she turned around to yell, "So long,
David. Good luck beating that rape charge."
Everyone onboard had turned to stare at me. Some
seemed curious, some seemed frightened, but the
overwhelming majority appeared to hate me with a
passion I had never before encountered. "That's my
sister," I'd said. "She likes to joke around." ("Picka
Pocketoni" 226)

The bond may also stem from Amy's having been—as
both slender and pretty—the one daughter to meet Lou's

demands. ("Look at you, you're the size of a house" ["A Shiner Like a Diamond" 133].) After all, it's hard for boys to value girls their father won't—even an abusive father.

Their bond now concerns the impressive way that Amy—as a New Yorker—will reject those demands: "getting even without first getting mad." Still slender, Amy once wore a fat suit home for the holidays. Sedaris went along for the ride, both figuratively and literally. Lou met the two of them at the airport. Visibly shaken, he said nothing on the way to the house. But the moment Amy stepped into the bathroom, he shouted: "What the hell happened to her? Christ almighty, this is killing me! I'm in real pain here."

> "What?"
>
> "Your sister, that's what. I just saw her six months ago, and now the girl's the size of a tank! I thought you were supposed to be keeping an eye on her."
>
> I begged him to lower his voice. "Please, Dad, don't mention it in front of her. Amy's very sensitive about her . . . you know."
>
> "Her what? Go ahead and say it: *her big, fat ass.* That's what she's ashamed of, and she should be! You could land a chopper on an ass like that."
>
> "Oh, Dad."
>
> "Don't try to defend her, wiseguy. She's a single woman, and the clock is ticking away. Who's going to love her, who's going to marry her with an ass like that?"

Still pretty, Amy appeared in an article on interesting New Yorkers looking like someone beat the crap out of her:

> The makeup artist did a fine job. The black eyes and purple jaw were accentuated by an

arrangement of scratch marks on her forehead. Pus-yellow pools girdled her scabbed nose, and her swollen lips were fenced with mean rows of brackish stitches.

Amy adored the disguise—as she had when apparently fat—and so, following her photo shoot, wore these bruises to the dry cleaner and then the grocery store. Most people looked away. But whenever someone asked what happened, she'd smile as brightly as possible, saying, "I'm in love. Can you believe it? I'm finally, totally in love, and I feel great" ("A Shiner Like a Diamond" 133, 137–38, 140–41, emphasis and ellipsis original).

This talent—this perversion, rather—goes way back. As a child, Amy was "Sybil with a better sense of humor, Eve without the crying jags." (The references are to the multiple personalities upon whom *The Three Faces of Eve* [1957], with Joanne Woodward, and then *Sybil* [1976], with Sally Field, were based.)

> "And who are we today?" my mother used to ask, leading to Amy's "Who don't you want me to be?" ("A Shiner Like a Diamond" 134)

As an adult, she was that battered woman. Or she's Jerri Blank on *Strangers with Candy*. Jerri—both created and performed by Amy—is a repulsive, lesbianic, and drug-addicted not-so-former prostitute (or as she puts it, "a boozer, a user, and a loser") who, at forty-six, moves back home to finish high school. (As such, she really messed up— much more so than Lisa, Tiffany, and Sedaris. Her mother, too, is dead. Her father, comatose. And as Jerri, Amy wears that fat suit.) The talent, moreover, is Sharon-related. It enabled Amy—like Sedaris now—to impersonate her:

> She became a Girl Scout only to become her Girl Scout leader. For Christmas and birthdays

she requested wigs and makeup, hospital gowns
and uniforms. Amy became my mother, and
then my mother's friends. ("A Shiner Like a
Diamond" 134)

And it's a talent the two of them shared. Sharon, you recall, was a "better actor" than Sedaris—in *Hamlet*—could
ever hope to be ("The Drama Bug" 105). Beyond "getting even," then, the bond between Amy and Sedaris now
concerns the fact that she—for him—is the one sister to
approximate their mother as both friend and—no, not lesbian. Both friend and thespian. Or rather, both friend and
star. Think: Sandra Church as Gypsy Rose Lee.

Amy's not, however, the furthest from Lou. That
would be Tiffany, who ran away at fourteen. Following
capture, he had her put in juvenile detention and then
sent to a school where punishment consisted of lying on
the floor while counselors hit golf balls into your mouth.
Basically, the place "restrained you until you were eighteen and allowed to run away legally." By that point, Tiffany
had developed both an aversion to Lou—understandably
enough—and an interest in baking. Following release,
she went to cooking school in Boston and then worked "in
the sort of restaurant that thought it amusing to flavor
brownies with tarragon and black pepper" ("Put a Lid on
It" 192, 193). Then, unfortunately, she lost the job.

Despite or possibly because of this aversion, Tiffany
also developed—in recent years—a curious habit. "Daddy's
been thinking about things a little too hard," she teased
Sedaris during a cab ride from his Boston hotel to her
Somerville apartment:

> "Daddy?"
> "Yeah," she said. "You."
> "Nobody calls me Daddy."
> "Mamma does."

"This is her new thing," Sedaris explains. "All men are called Daddy, and all women, Mamma. At the age of forty she talks like a far-sighted baby." Upon arrival, though, things got ugly. He sensed Tiffany bracing herself against what she saw as his inevitable judgment—not so much articulated by Sedaris, as implied in large part by the example he'd always set. "I haven't had a chance to clean," she said, but the lie felt uncomfortable, and so she corrected herself. "What I meant to say is that I don't give a fuck what you think of my apartment. I didn't really want you here in the first place." He was supposed to feel good that Tiffany got this off her chest. But it hurt to know that, should he ask, his sister would say exactly how much she'd been dreading this visit. So he didn't ask, commenting instead on the cat brushing up against the porch rails. "Oh," she said. "That's Daddy." Then she took off her shoes and opened the door ("Put a Lid on It" 190, 198).

Once inside, Sedaris tried to ignore what he saw as squalor, doing pretty well until they hit the kitchen:

> The last time I visited, Tiffany was pulling up the linoleum. I'd assumed that this was part of a process, phase one to be followed by phase two. It hadn't occurred to me that this was a one-step procedure, the final product a tar-paper floor. Combine it with bare feet and you're privy to the pedicurist's worst nightmare. My sister has appendages connected to her ankles. They feature toes and arches, but I cannot call them feet. In color they resemble the leathery paws of great apes, but in texture they are closer to hooves. In order to maintain her balance, she'll periodically clear the bottoms of debris—a bottle cap, bits of broken glass, a chicken bone—but within moments she'll have stepped on something else and begun the process

all over again. It's what happens when you sell both your broom and your vacuum cleaner.

Jerri has the same feet. At any rate:

> I see the dirty rag covering the lower half of the kitchen window, the crusted broken-handled pans scattered across the greasy stovetop. My sister is living in a Dorothy Lange photograph, and the homosexual in me wants to get down and scrub until my fingers bleed. I'd done it on all my previous visits, hoping each time that it might make some kind of impression. Gleaming appliances, a bathroom reeking of bleach: "Doesn't this smell great!" I'd say. The last time I was here, after scraping, cleaning, and waxing her living-room floor, I watched as she overturned a wineglass onto what amounted to six hours' worth of work. It wasn't an accident, but a deliberate statement: I do not want what you have to offer. She later phoned my brother, referring to me as Fairy Poppins, which wouldn't bother me if it weren't so apt. ("Put a Lid on It" 199–200)

Not surprisingly, the mess this Mamma's made of her life was both literal and figurative. She'd been out of work a long time. She'd become nocturnal. And she spent most of the night scavenging:

> These days while the rest of the world sleeps, my sister goes through their garbage. She carries a flashlight and a pair of rubber gloves and comes across a surprising number of teeth. ("Put a Lid on It" 195)

But Tiffany *sounds* good, which Lou thinks means she should sing. "She's got a beautiful voice," he says. "I just wish to hell she'd *do* something with it." Asked what that might be, he says she should put out an album. "But she doesn't sing," says Sedaris.

> "Well, she *could*." He speaks as if not releasing an album is just laziness on her part, as if people just walk in off the street, lay down a dozen or so tracks, and hand them over to eager radio stations. I've never heard Tiffany sing so much as "Happy Birthday," but when it comes to speaking, my father is right—she does have a beautiful voice. Even when she was a child it was smoky and full-bodied, lending even her most banal statements a cunning, slightly sexual undertone.

"A person needs to use their best assets," says Lou. "If she doesn't want to put out an album, she could maybe be a receptionist. All she'd have to do is answer the damned phone." But Tiffany isn't looking for career advice, writes Sedaris, "especially from our father" ("Put a Lid on It" 191–92, emphasis original).

And things she makes now *look* good, which Sedaris thinks means Tiffany should sell. "I've been doing a lot of tile work," she told him in the kitchen:

> I follow her finger in the direction of the refrigerator, where a mosaic panel leans against the wall. She started making them a few years ago, using the bits of broken crockery she finds in the trash. Her latest project is the size of a bath mat and features the remains of a Hummel figurine, the once cherubic face now reeling in a vortex of shattered coffee mugs. Like the elaborate gingerbread houses she made during her baking days, Tiffany's mosaics reflect the loopy energy of someone who will simply die if she doesn't express

herself. It's a rare quality, and because it requires an absolute lack of self-consciousness, she is unable to see it.

"A woman offered to buy it," she said, surprised someone else took an interest. "We set a price, but then, I don't know, I feel wrong accepting that kind of money" ("Put a Lid on It" 201).

Sedaris could understand thinking you're not good enough, but no one needs cash more than Tiffany. "You could sell it and buy a vacuum cleaner," he suggested. "Lay some new linoleum on the floor, wouldn't that be nice?"

"What is it with you and my kitchen floor?" she asks. "Who cares about the goddam linoleum?"

In the corner of the room Daddy approaches my sports coat, kneading it with his paws before lying down and curling into a ball. "I don't know why I even bother with you," Tiffany says. She'd wanted to show me her artwork—something that truly interests her, something she's good at—and instead, like my father, I'm suggesting she become an entirely different person.

Like Lou, that is, he was being selfish—self-centered, rather. Like Lou, this Daddy's ashamed to admit, he couldn't fathom that things important to him weren't important to Tiffany as well. He couldn't not come off sounding like a missionary, someone whose job it is to convert rather than to listen. *"Yes, your Tiki god is very handsome, but we're here to talk about Jesus."* Even when silent, and even without having cleaned this time, he seemed to broadcast prissy disapproval, comparing the woman Tiffany is with some woman she'll never be—a sanitized version who leaves other people's teeth where she finds them. No wonder she dreads his visits. No wonder she dislikes both Lou and Sedaris. No wonder she's distant from the two of them ("Put a Lid on It" 202–3).

As with most Sedaris, this satire—"Put a Lid on It"—is both sanguine and cynical. As cynical satire, moreover, it's a *confession*. As sanguine satire, it says—to Lou, primarily: shame on you for having done this to Tiffany. (It doesn't, however, shame Tiffany.) As confession, it says to her: shame on *me* for doing pretty much the same. (For more on the topic of confession, please see "André," this volume.) In addition to "wounding," "punishing," or "destroying" Sedaris himself, that is, the essay apologizes—rather directly—for having been an asshole during all those trips to Massachusetts (Highet 235). It's an explanation as well. Neither Sedaris nor their father, he'd have her understand, dislikes Tiffany. Neither wants distance from her. Neither one is mean. It's just that, without a regular job and the right linoleum, they're both worried "she'll fall through a crack and disappear to a place where we can't find her" ("Put a Lid on It" 203). The question remains, though: should Sedaris also apologize to Tiffany for having just revealed so much about her—for having *published* that essay?

The answer—*yes,* of course—comes in an essay about a trip to North Carolina. We already know that Lisa, like Sharon, is benevolent. It's she who brought that prostitute home (see "Dinah, the Christmas Whore"). We know that, unlike Sharon, she's sentimental. It's Lisa who could tell a parent, *I love you* (see "Ashes" 240). We also know she's the next most insulting after Paul. Lisa called Sedaris an asshole just before abandoning him at summer camp. "Listen, asshole," she said. "As far as this place is concerned, I don't know you and you sure as shit don't know me, you got that?" ("I Like Guys" 88). She called Sharon a bitch—though not to her face—just after having been locked out of the house (see "Let It Snow" 14). She told Lou something even worse after getting her first period at a golf tournament:

> The game finally over, we returned to the parking lot to find Lisa stretched out in the backseat of the Porsche, her face and lap covered with golf towels.
>
> "Don't say it," she threatened. "Whatever it is, I don't want to hear it."
>
> "All I was going to do was ask you to take your lousy feet off the seat of the car," my father said.
>
> "Yeah, well, why don't you go fuck yourself."
> ("The Women's Open" 58)

We're now told that she loves pets. (So did Sharon. [See "Me Talk Pretty One Day" 169, on cats; "The Youth in Asia" 69–82, on dogs.]) Both other people's pets, including strangers':

> Lisa's a person who once witnessed a car accident, saying, "I just hope there isn't a dog in the backseat." Human suffering doesn't faze her much, but she'll cry for days over a sick-pet story. ("Repeat After Me" 151)

And of course her own—Henry in particular. Henry's a parrot, a blue-fronted Amazon then situated—at the beginning of the visit—in Lisa's kitchen and, for the moment, repeatedly asking in her voice: *How you doing? How you doing? How you doing?* Sedaris could understand this attachment: his sister loves the devotion, the doglike loyalty to her alone. She also loves the attention, the motherly yet self-directed interest. "Here was this strange little fatso . . . a sympathetic listener turning again and again to ask, 'So, really, how are you?'" Unfortunately, it had no idea what this meant:

When she first got him, Henry spoke the Spanish he'd learned from his captors. Asked if he'd had a good night's sleep, he'd say simply, "*Hola,*" or "*Bueno.*" He goes through phases, favoring an often repeated noise or sentence, and then moving on to something else. When our mother died, Henry learned to cry. He and Lisa would set each other off, and the two of them would go on for hours. A few years later, in the midst of a brief academic setback, she trained him to act as her emotional cheerleader. I'd call and hear him in the background, screaming, "We love you, Lisa!" and "You can do it!"

This had been replaced, in time, with the far more practical "Where are my keys?" ("Repeat After Me" 146, 147, 149–50).

The reason Sedaris has told—or written—so much about Lisa, much more than about any other sister, is not that she's his only older and therefore maternal one. Nor is it that she made an even bigger mess of her life than either Tiffany or Sedaris. (Like Sedaris, Lisa dropped out of college and moved back home. Unlike him, she got a job and then her own apartment. Unlike Tiffany, she's still employed and sufficiently clean. *Schadenfreude,* then, is almost completely out of the question.) It's that her mess alone concerned all of them. To his relational—or structural—way of thinking:

> As children we'd been assigned certain roles—leader, bum, troublemaker, slut—titles that effectively told us who we were. As the oldest, smartest, and bossiest, it was naturally assumed that Lisa would shoot to the top of her field, earning a master's degree in manipulation and eventually taking over a medium-sized country.

And if the oldest wasn't who she was supposed to be, "then what did that mean for the rest of us?" In fact, to his both relational and *oppositional*—also self-centered—way of thinking, the mess concerned Sedaris in particular. For a mental—also structural—picture of oppositionality, think: yin and yang. *Yin:* As the least "lazy and irresponsible" sibling, Lisa would succeed in life. *Yang:* As the laziest and least responsible, Sedaris would therefore fail. No wonder Sedaris had been especially "disoriented" by Lisa's fall, even while taking a certain joy in watching it (*schaden-freude*). Not to mention annoyed or irritated—as with Sharon and that vacuum: "More often than not," Sedaris writes, "I found myself wanting to shake her" ("Repeat After Me" 143–44).

Every sibling, however, is annoyed by Sedaris—even Amy. In his mind, he's a "friendly junkman." In mine, he's a Tiffany-like scavenger—building things from the little pieces of scrap he finds here and there. The siblings, how-ever, see things differently:

> Their personal lives are the so-called pieces of scrap
> I so casually pick up, and they're sick of it. More
> and more often their stories begin with the line
> "You have to swear you will never repeat this." I
> always promise, but it's generally understood that
> my word means nothing.

Given how much more he's written about her, Lisa—understandably enough—is especially annoyed. She's fear-ful as well, "afraid to tell me anything important" ("Repeat After Me" 147). These are related facts of which Sedaris, back in North Carolina, had been aware for quite some time. But he was about to realize, in a relatively selfless epiphany, yet another basis of Lisa's fear and irritation. He was about to realize—possibly at the end of the visit, possibly thereafter, probably while writing "Repeat After

Me"—another reason she's "sick of it": Lisa alone, of all
the siblings, not only disoriented but disappointed herself. Not only was being a dropout not what anyone else
had planned for her, it wasn't what *she* had. And as bad
as that failure—that shameful failure—had been for the
rest of them, Sedaris in particular, it was so much worse
for Lisa. (Recall Probyn: "That little moment of disappointment is amplified into shame or a deep disappointment in ourselves" [13].) So it's nothing she herself really
cares to read about—repeatedly. Our reading about it—
both repeatedly and, in a sense, in public—must feel to
her like abuse.

That realization was prompted by Lisa, against her
better judgment, having told Sedaris something too good—
too benevolent, really—for him not to publish. They'd just
seen *You Can Count on Me* (2000), the presumably autobiographical film about a brother and sister who, "like
us, [had] stumbled into adulthood playing the worn, con-
fining roles assigned to them as children." Lisa parked in
front of her house, then turned to relate what Sedaris
would "come to think of as the quintessential Lisa story."
It seems to have been about a dog, probably killed—by
Lisa—after an accident she herself caused. For reasons I'll
get to, we're not told for sure:

> "One time," she began, "one time I was out driving?"
> The incident began with a quick trip to the grocery
> store and ended, unexpectedly, with a wounded
> animal stuffed into a pillowcase and held to the
> tailpipe of her car. Like most of my sister's stories,
> it provoked a startling mental picture, capturing a
> moment in time when one's actions seem both
> unimaginably cruel and completely natural. Details
> were carefully chosen and the pace built gradually,
> punctuated by a series of well-timed pauses. "And

then . . . and then . . ." She reached the inevitable conclusion and just as I started to laugh, she put her head against the steering wheel and fell apart. It wasn't the gentle flow of tears you might release when recalling an isolated action or event, but the violent explosion that comes when you realize that all such events are connected, forming an endless chain of guilt and suffering.

Or guilt, suffering, and disappointment. For not only did that "chain" include other such accidents and euthanasias, and not only did it include the loss of Sharon, it also—I imagine Sedaris imagining, in that epiphany— included both Lisa's quitting college and everything that happened to her in its wake. Maybe even, though it sounds ridiculous, the loss of keys. At any rate, Sedaris reached for a notebook. And then Lisa grabbed his hand. "If you ever," she said, "*ever* repeat that story, I will never talk to you again." In a film about their own lives, Sedaris does imagine, he would have comforted Lisa at this point, "reminding her, convincing her that the action she'd described had been kind and just." In reality, his immediate, selfish goal was simply to change her mind. "Oh, come on," he said. "The story's really funny, and, I mean, it's not like *you're* going to do anything with it" ("Repeat After Me" 153, 154–55, emphasis and ellipses original).

By the way, Sedaris himself had been involved in another such accident. One rainy night, shortly after he got his learner's permit, Sharon picked Sedaris up from a play rehearsal—probably *Hamlet*—and then, cresting a hill, ran over something she shouldn't have. "'Shit,' my mother whispered, tapping her forehead against the steering wheel. 'Shit, shit, shit.'" They covered their heads against the rain and then searched the street. There it was, an orange cat coughing up blood into the gutter:

"You killed me," the cat said, pointing at my mother with its flattened paw. "Here I had so much to live for, but now it's over, my whole life wiped out just like that." The cat wheezed rhythmically before closing its eyes and dying.

"Shit," my mother repeated. We walked door to door until finding the cat's owner, a kind and understanding woman whose young daughter shared none of her qualities. "You killed my cat," she screamed, sobbing into her mother's skirt. "You're mean and ugly and you killed my cat."

"She's at that age," the woman said, stroking the child's hair.

My mother felt bad enough without the lecture that awaited her at home. "That could have been a child!" my father shouted. "Think about that the next time you're tearing down the street searching for kicks." He made it sound as if my mother ran down cats for sport. "You think this is funny," he said, "but we'll see who's laughing when you're behind bars awaiting trial for manslaughter." ("Cyclops" 50–51)

Sedaris would receive a variation on the same abusive speech—once again, from Lou—after hitting a mailbox. And so, despite Sharon's encouragement, he never drove again. Nor, as far as we know, has he ever made the connection: Sharon-as-traumatized-cat-killer, Lisa-as-dog-killer. At least, not consciously.

At any rate, the next thing we're shown this "small, evil man" doing is turning to his sister, still sobbing, and asking, "What if I use the story but say that it happened to a friend?" Sedaris, here, begins describing himself in the third person, self-consciously cinematic narration that will end the essay. *Fade out. Fade in.* And then—in the film of their lives, if not reality—Sedaris (played by Amy, perhaps) gets out of bed, walks past Lisa's room, and continues downstairs to the kitchen. He then approaches a large birdcage covered with a tablecloth, removes the cloth, and begins training Henry—in *his* voice—to ask or perhaps demand something other than *How you doing:*

> From his own mouth the words are meaningless, and so he pulls up a chair. The clock reads three A.M., then four, then five, as he sits before the brilliant bird, repeating slowly and clearly the words "Forgive me. Forgive me. Forgive me."
> ("Repeat After Me" 155, 156)

Forgive Sedaris, that is, for his behavior in the car. Forgive him for having published all those essays. Forgive him for publishing this one, which unlike "Put a Lid on It"—by not revealing too much, not repeating (at least, not verbatim, or in any detail) that story about what seems to have been a dog—will also have apologized for itself.

"Forgive me. Forgive me. Forgive me." When Lou kicked Sedaris out, you recall, Sharon cried until it sounded as if she were choking. "I'm sorry," she said. "I'm sorry, I'm sorry, I'm sorry" ("Hejira" 89). *Forgive me, Forgive me, Forgive me*; *I'm sorry, I'm sorry, I'm sorry*—another connection Sedaris may never make. After all—aside from the fact that the "performative" *Forgive me,* like *I love you,* is too demanding to be utterly unselfish or maternal, not to mention too formal to sound like Sharon; aside, moreover, from the fact that it wasn't Sharon but Lou who should have apologized—what's the difference? (By *performative,* once again, I don't mean theatrical. I mean speech acts—like *I apologize* or even *Shame on you*—that when done correctly both say and do things, either confirm or transform relationships.) What's the difference, really, between this "Forgive me" and that "I'm sorry," or between Sedaris now and Sharon then?

Paul

The night "the Rooster" was born, Sedaris recalls, "my father slipped into my bedroom to personally deliver the news."

> I was eleven years old and barely awake, yet still I recognized this as a supreme masculine moment: the patriarch informing his firstborn son that another player was joining the team. Looking around my room, at the vase of cattails arranged just so beside the potpourri bowl, he should have realized it was not his team I was playing for. Not even a girl would have découpaged her own electrical sockets, but finding it too painful to consider, my father played through, going so far as to offer a plastic-wrapped cigar, the band reading IT'S A BOY.

He, Sedaris, would rather Paul weren't:

For the first six months, my brother, Paul, was just a blob, then a doll my sisters and I could diaper and groom as we saw fit. Dress him appropriately and it was easy to forget the tiny penis lying like a canned mushroom between his legs. Given some imagination and a few well-chosen accessories, he was Paulette, the pouty French girl; Paola, the dark-wigged *bambina* fresh from her native Tuscany; Pauline, the swinging hippie chick. As a helpless infant, he went along with it, but by the age of eighteen months he'd effectively dispelled the theory that a person can be made gay. Despite our best efforts, the cigar band had been right. Our brother was a boy. He inherited my sports equipment, still in its original wrapping, and took to the streets with actual friends, playing whatever was in season: If he won, great, and if he lost, big deal.

"But aren't you going to weep?" his siblings would ask. "Not even a little?" They tried explaining the benefits of a nice long cry—"the release it offered, the pity it generated"—and Paul laughed in their faces. While the rest of them "blubbered like leaky showerheads," his water production was limited to sweat and urine ("Rooster at the Hitchin' Post" 165, 166).

Paul, then, is both masculine and happy. So much so, in fact, that it's always "all about the joke" for him—regardless of the situation. And much as they tell Sedaris stories even knowing that his promise not to publish will have meant nothing, the rest of them—in moments of weakness—fall for such setups as a warm embrace by Paul or a heartfelt declaration of concern even after having repeatedly promised themselves never to do so. For example, the last time Sedaris accepted a hug he then flew from Raleigh to New York both miserable and oblivious of the sign his brother had slapped to the back of his sports coat: a sticker reading, *Hello, I'm Gay.* "This," he adds, "following the hilarity of our mother's funeral" ("Rooster at the Hitchin' Post" 166, 167). This, moreover, wasn't really teasing—or at least, unlike Amy's "Good luck beating that rape charge" on the train, not the time or place for it ("Picka Pocketoni" 226).

Despite these differences of gender, sexuality, sentimentality, and now class, Sedaris loves Paul. So much so, in fact, that he shouldn't find him ridiculous. Only snobs would—for which we, Sedaris included, should be ashamed of ourselves. (Paul, you recall, consorts with men who proffer such advice as, "If she's old enough to bleed, she's old enough to breed" ["You Can't Kill the Rooster" 67].) He loves Paul, moreover, like a father—découpage be damned. Proust, by contrast, loved his brother—younger by only two years—like a mother. "As far back in my recollections of childhood at that period, when one's earliest memories begin to crystallize, I constantly have before me the image of my brother watching over me with a sweetness that is infinite, enveloping and, so to speak, maternal," Robert recalled in eulogy.

> For me he always had the fraternal and watchful
> attitude of an older person, but additionally I sensed
> in him traces of our dear departed ones and up until
> the last he always remained for me much more
> than the guardian of these mental relics; he was my
> entire past; my whole youth was locked away inside
> his unique personality. (Quoted in Tadié 39)

This tells us something about gay sexuality—as opposed to the homosexuality or "inversion" of yesteryear.

Paul, however, already has a father—to him a rather good one. No wonder every time Sedaris is about to say something like *I love you, son*—or even *I'm proud of you*—the Rooster cuts him off with something like their mother's *I'll pretend I didn't hear that* ("Ashes" 240). (Real fathers, to avoid both sentimentality and queerness, express not love but "pride." So do would-be ones—even, or especially, if gay. But of course "it was queer" for Sedaris to have said *I love you* to Sharon ["Ashes" 240].) When Sedaris was twenty-three, for example, the two were horsing around at Atlantic Beach. Finding themselves on the wrong side of the waves, drifting farther and farther from their hotel, Sedaris swam for shore. Paul, he thought, was right behind him:

> He wasn't supposed to be out at that time of day, especially with me. "You wind him up," my mother said. "For God's sake, just give it a rest." When accused of winding up my sisters, I'd always felt a hint of shame, but I liked the fact that I could adequately enthuse a twelve-year-old boy. As an older brother, it was my job, and I liked to think that I was good at it. I swam for what felt like the length of a pool and turned around. But Paul wasn't there.
> A swell moved in, and my brother went under, leaving only his right arm, which waved the international sign language for "I am going to die now and it is all your fault." I headed back in his direction, trying to recall the water-safety class years earlier at the country club. *Think,* I told myself. *Think like a man.* I tried to focus, but all that came to me was the instructor, an athletic seventeen-year-old named Chip Pancake. I remembered the spray of freckles on his broad, bronzed shoulders and my small rush of hope as he searched the assembled students for a resuscitation victim. *Oh, choose me,* I'd whispered. *Me! Over here.* I recalled the smell of hamburgers drifting from the

clubhouse, the sting of the life jacket against my
sunburned back, and the crushing disappointment
I felt when Chip selected Patsy Pyle, who would
later describe the experience as "life-changing."
These are not the sorts of memories that save
lives, so I abandoned the past and relied instead
upon instinct.

Sedaris then grabbed Paul by the hair and yelled at him
to lie flat. Then they kicked their way back to the beach,
washing ashore a good half mile from the hotel. Lying
side by side, catching their breath in the shallow surf,
it seemed a moment when something should be said, by
Sedaris, some declaration of relief and "brotherly love."
(For "brotherly," though, read *fatherly*.) "Listen," he began.
"I just want you to know . . ." "Fuck you," Paul said
("Rooster at the Hitchin' Post" 175–77, ellipsis original).

When Sedaris was forty-five, Paul got married at
the same hotel. Lou, waving a rubber chicken, delivered
a very awkward toast. "I cannot believe you," Sedaris
snapped. "A rubber *chicken?*" Lou claimed he couldn't find
a rooster. Sedaris explained that wasn't really the point.
"Not everyone has the ability to improvise," he said.
"Where were your notes? Why didn't you come to me for
help?" Sedaris now explains, primarily to Paul, that if he
was "hard" on Lou—abusive perhaps—it was out of envy.
He, Sedaris, should have been best man. He should have
given the toast. He'd been planning on it since Paul was a
boy, but nobody had asked ("Rooster at the Hitchin' Post"
177, emphasis original).

After the reception, Paul took his dogs Diesel (a Great
Dane) and Venus (a pug) for a walk. Sedaris went along.
It was the first time the brothers had been alone since
the ceremony, and Sedaris, once again, "wanted to force a
moment out of it"—the kind of masculine and presumably

patriarchal one that his "I just want you to know . . ." on the beach would have been, also the kind his toast would have been. The operative word, he writes, is *force,* because "it never works that way." In trying to be memorable, "you wind up sounding unspeakably queer"—or formal, perhaps—"which may be remembered but never the way you'd hoped." Luckily, Paul "had spent his life saving me from such moments."

> A light rain began to fall, and just as I cleared my throat, Venus squatted in the grass, producing a mound of peanut-sized turds.
> "Aren't you going to clean that up?" I asked.
> Paul pointed to the ground and whistled for the Great Dane, which thundered across the lawn and ate the feces in one bite.
> "Tell me that was an accident," I said.
> "Accident, hell. I got this motherfucker *trained,*" he said. "Sometimes he'll stick his nose to her ass and just eat that shit on tap."

Sedaris thought of Paul standing in his backyard and training a dog to eat shit and realized he'd probably think about it until the day he dies. "Forget the tears and brotherly speeches, this was the stuff that memories are made of." (For "brotherly," once again, read *fatherly.*) Diesel then licked his lips and searched the grass for more. "What was it you were going to say?" Paul asked. "Oh, nothing," said Sedaris ("Rooster at the Hitchin' Post" 177, 178, emphasis original).

Sedaris may never say anything like *I love you, son*— let alone, unlike Lisa, those exact words. But to the extent they address Paul, the essays "You Can't Kill the Rooster," "Rooster at the Hitchin' Post," and "Baby Einstein" say it for him. Or rather, they show it—much as "Repeat After Me" apologized. They demonstrate the emotion without, I

imagine, demanding anything filial in return. Anything
from Paul, that is. All three demand something of readers
egalitarian enough to identify with him. "Baby Einstein,"
moreover, demands something of Paul's own firstborn,
the then infant daughter of whom he's proud, in relation
to whom he's surprisingly maternal, and to whom the
essay is also addressed. It demands or at least suggests
that she, too, love him.

"My sister-in-law's condition calls for her to sleep
through the night," Sedaris concludes, "so when Madelyn
wakes at two and three and five A.M., it is Paul's job to
feed her or change her, or carry her around the house, beg-
ging her to lighten up."

> There's no point going to bed, so he kicks his pillow
> from room to room and collapses on the floor in
> front of her crib or the swinging chair that sits in
> the dining room. When the last of my sisters has
> hit the sack, he dials me up and holds the receiver
> to his daughter's mouth. For months I listened to
> her cry long-distance, but then she got a little older
> and learned how to laugh and coo and sigh in that
> satisfied baby way that makes me understand how
> some could bring a child into this lousy world of ours.

"In a couple of years," says Lou, "Madelyn won't want anything to do with him." So Sedaris looks into the future.
There's Paul, impossibly middle-aged. And there's Madelyn, the valedictorian of a major university. What will she
think, he wonders, when Paul stands in the aisle, releases
a hog call, and lifts his T-shirt to reveal some jiggling
message painted on his stomach? Will she turn away, as
Lou predicts? Or—perhaps not so impossible—will she
remember all those nights she awoke to find "this slob,
this lump, this silly drooling toy asleep at her feet" ("Baby
Einstein" 244–45).

Mrs. Colgate

Sedaris had awful teachers in both elementary and middle school. His third-grade teacher, Miss Chestnut, tried to shame him—abusively and in public—out of obsessive-compulsive behavior:

> According to her calculations, I had left my chair twenty-eight times that day. "You're up and down like a flea. I turn my back for two minutes and there you are with your tongue pressed against that light switch. Maybe they do that where you come from, but here in my classroom we don't leave our seats and lick things whenever we please. That is Miss Chestnut's light switch, and she likes to keep it dry. Would you like me to come over to your house and put my tongue on *your* light switches? Well, would you?" ("A Plague of Tics" 7, emphasis original)

The attempt was unsuccessful. He's still compulsive.

His fifth-grade speech therapist, Miss Samson, tried—
in private—to shame him out of a lisp. The attempt, once
again, was unsuccessful. Nor did any therapy ever since
make a difference. The only difference then was that he
became quieter and morbidly self-conscious. (This, perhaps,
was where Sedaris lost the "loopy energy" Tiffany couldn't
know she's got ["Put a Lid on It" 201].) Thanks to Miss
Samson's tape recorder, he now had "a clear sense of what
[he] actually sounded like."

> There was the lisp, of course, but more troubling
> was my voice itself, with its excitable tone and
> high, girlish pitch. I'd hear myself ordering lunch
> in the cafeteria, and the sound would turn my
> stomach. How could anyone stand to listen to me?

If only this inexperienced young woman—clearly, in ret-
rospect, just out of college—had "acted friendly" ("Go
Carolina" 12, 15). If only, like Henry, she'd been more
cheerleader than drill sergeant. Sedaris, you recall, would
hear the bird scream, "We love you, Lisa!" and "You can do
it!" ("Repeat After Me" 149).

Proust, incidentally, seems to have been treated by—
or least to have treated—all teachers as "equals" (Tadié
66). Then again, he hadn't attended the French equivalent
of a public school. According to one classmate:

> The Lycée Condorcet was never a prison. In those
> days [the 1880s], it was like a sort of inner circle,
> whose appeal was so subtle that certain pupils—
> Marcel Proust, for instance, and my other friends—
> often did their best to arrive before the time we
> were officially meant to be there: so impatient were
> we to see one another again and chat beneath the
> sparse shade of the trees that adorned the Havre
> courtyard, while we waited the rolling of the drum,

which advised us, rather than commanded us, that
we should make our way to the classrooms. The
discipline was not harsh, it even struck our families
as being a little too relaxed. (Robert Dreyfus,
quoted in Tadié 55)

Proust's narrator, in another paralipsis, doesn't mention
the experience.

The seventh-grade English teacher was an improve-
ment, for Sedaris. Like Sharon, she used shame—or perhaps teasing—to nurture, to rid Sedaris of a "wretched
eagerness to please" (*Children Playing before a Statue of
Hercules,* 3).

> One afternoon, in the middle of a particularly
> boring grammar lesson, my seventh-grade English
> teacher set aside her book and took nominations
> for the best song on WKIX, our local Top 40 radio
> station. It was her way of getting the circulation
> back into our arms, and it worked like a charm.
> For the first time that year, all hands were in the
> air, not just at head level, but well above it, and
> waving, as if they held flags. There was no "right
> answer" to a question of personal taste, or so I
> thought until she eventually called on me, and
> I announced that "Indiana Wants Me" was not only
> the best song in the Top 40 but possibly the best
> song ever. The phrase "in the history of all time"
> may have been used, but what I remember is not
> my recommendation so much as the silence that
> followed it, an absence of agreement I can only
> describe as deafening.
>
> The person in front of me, a guy named
> Teetsil, turned around in his seat. "'Indiana Wants
> Me'?"
>
> "Now, now," the teacher said, "to each his own."

Teetsil said that was fine or whatever. "But *'Indiana Wants Me'*? He's got to be kidding."

Sedaris wasn't friends with Teetsil. No one was. But on hearing the boy's disapproval, he decided that maybe his choice wasn't all it was cracked up to be. "I thought I'd enjoyed it as a grim little narrative, the confession of a man who was wanted for murder in the exotic Midwest. The singer's voice was tinged with regret, more country than pop, and that, too, I liked, or thought I had." (This description—a "grim little narrative," a "confession [in which] the singer's voice [is] tinged with regret"—would apply to almost any Sedaris essay. His sanguine satire says *shame on you;* his cynical or perhaps lyrical satire, *shame on me.*) The song, in fact, had satisfied Sedaris on every level. But if nobody else liked it, then he didn't either. "What I meant," he now said, "is that I *don't* like 'Indiana Wants Me.' My sister does, she plays it all the time, but me, I can't stand it."

"Then what *do* you like?" the teacher asked, and I saw the same expression our cat had when torturing a mole.

I looked at Teetsil, who'd named something by the Rolling Stones, and then at the girl across the aisle who liked the Carpenters.

"Everything," I announced, "I like everything."

"Everything but 'Indiana Wants Me'?"

"Yes," I said. "Everything but that."

This didn't work either, perhaps because also done in public. And it took another twenty years for Sedaris to stop conforming to the will of others and start distinguishing, if only as a reader, "between what I enjoyed and what I thought I should" (1–2, 4, emphasis original).

Sedaris doesn't name that English teacher. In "Jamboree," though, she's "Mrs. Colgate"—a kind woman who tells Chug to "read, read, read" as well as keep in touch. The one time he does call, however, she answers: "For the love of God, Curtis, I can explain everything" (103). Chug hangs up. We're not told if Curtis is Mr. Colgate, or if he's a lover. How would Chug know?

Lou forced him to learn guitar at about the same time. (Like golf, jazz was an obsession. Music lessons were therefore imposed much as tournament attendance had been—regardless of one's aversion.) Sedaris was twelve. Mr. Mancini, the teacher, was a midget. He was cool, too, but homophobic. When Sedaris finally admitted both that he'd no interest in the instrument and that what he really wanted was to sing commercials in the voice of Billie Holiday—*Thaaaat Os-carrr May-errr has a way, with B-Oooo-L-Oooo-G-N-A,* he'd impersonate—Mr. Mancini held up his hands as if to stop a car. "Hey, guy," he said. "You can hold it right there. I'm not into that scene." What scene? Sedaris thought he was being original:

> "There were plenty of screwballs like you back in Atlanta, but me, I don't swing that way— you got it? This might be your 'thing' or whatever, but you can definitely count me out." He reached for his conch shell and stubbed out his cigarette. "I mean, come on now. For God's sake, kid; pull yourself together." ("Giant Dreams, Midget Abilities" 29)

He'd said *screwball,* but Sedaris knew what he really meant.

In "My Manuscript," Mr. Mancini—or "Chatam"—is both uncool and oblivious. According to Chad Holt, gay pornographer:

> Mr. Chatam sat perched on the edge of a footstool and wore outfits that a child might wear: checkered

suits with clip-on ties and buckled shoes. The guitar
was huge in his lap and I would almost feel sorry
for him until he opened his wee mouth to say
something stupid like "Here's a little number those
girlfriends of yours might enjoy hearing!" and he'd
force me to follow along as he played another
tiresome ballad from something called *The Young
Person's Contemporary Songbook.*

In Chad's manuscript, Mr. Chatam is kept in an orphan-
age, completely nude, his head and body shaved, until he
is adopted by a group of truck-driving studs for use as a
sex baby. Unlike most babies, however, Mr. Chatam loves
getting spanked. "And once he starts bawling there's only
one way to pacify him!" (24).

His Spanish teacher the following year—also unnamed—was both racist and narcissistic. When it was
announced that, come fall, their school system would adopt
a policy of racial integration by way of forced busing, the
woman broke the news "in a way she hoped might lead us
to a greater understanding of her beauty and generosity."

"I remember the time I was at the state fair,
standing in line for a Sno-Kone," she said, fingering
the kiss curls that framed her squat, compact face.
"And a little colored girl ran up and tugged at my
skirt, asking if she could touch my hair. 'Just once,'
she said. 'Just one time for good luck.'"

"Now, I don't know about the rest of you, but
my hair means a lot to me." The members of my
class nodded to signify that their hair meant a lot
to them as well. They inched forward in their seats,
eager to know where this story might be going.
Perhaps the little Negro girl was holding a
concealed razor blade. Maybe she was one of the
troublemakers out for a fresh white scalp.

Sedaris marveled at their naïveté. Like all the woman's anecdotes, this was headed "straight up her ass."

> "I checked to make sure she didn't have any candy on her hands, and then I bent down and let this little colored girl touch my hair." The teacher's eyes assumed the dewy, far-away look she reserved for such Hallmark moments. "Then this little fudge-colored girl put her hand on my cheek and said, 'Oh,' she said, 'I wish I could be white and pretty like you.'" She paused, positioning herself at the edge of her desk as though she were posing for a portrait the federal government might use on a stamp commemorating gallantry. "The thing to remember," she said, "is that more than anything in this world, those colored people wish they were white." ("I Like Guys" 81–82)

She's homophobic as well, like Mancini. This was the same teacher who when announcing her first pregnancy had said, "I'll have a boy and then maybe later I'll have a girl, because when you do it the other way round"— as Sharon had with Sedaris, after Lisa—"there's a good chance the boy will turn out to be funny." "'Funny,' as in having no arms and legs?" Sedaris asked:

> "That," the teacher said, "is far from funny. That is tragic, and you, sir, should have your lips sewn shut for saying such a cruel and ugly thing. When I say 'funny,' I mean funny as in . . ." She relaxed her wrist, allowing her hand to dangle and flop. "I mean 'funny' as in *that* kind of funny." She minced across the room, but it failed to illustrate her point, as this was more or less her natural walk, a series of gamboling little steps, her back held straight, giving the impression she was balancing something of value atop her empty head.

His math teacher at the time did a much better—hence crueler—impression. Snatching a purse from some girl, he'd prance about, bat his eyes, blow kisses at some boy, then say "fairy nice to meet you" ("I Like Guys" 82, emphasis and ellipsis original).

Having been abusively shamed by most of these teachers—the homophobes in particular—Sedaris, in return, shames them nonabusively. As a sanguine satirist, he both addresses and ridicules them as racist, narcissistic, homophobic, or just incompetent. *Spanks* them, rather—as with Mancini. Of course, it's thirty years too late—as is *Strangers with Candy*. And so, as that satirist, he also suggests or perhaps demands that readers egalitarian enough—or not too homophobic—to identify with Sedaris, gays in particular, reject this treatment. *Don't let what happened to me happen to you,* we're shown. *Shame such people immediately.*

Students in his own first class did just that. They did so, however, not in return for Sedaris having shamed them, at least not initially. Nor even because—it being impossible for him to write without a cigarette—he'd let them smoke. ("This, to me, was the very essence of teaching, and I thought I'd made a real breakthrough until the class asthmatic raised his hand, saying that, to the best of his knowledge, Aristophanes had never smoked a cigarette in his life" ["The Learning Curve" 86]. Troublemaker.) They shamed Sedaris because he was both inexperienced and—unlike Miss Samson—incompetent.

"A year after my graduation from the School of the Art Institute of Chicago," the confession begins, "a terrible mistake was made and I was offered a position teaching a writing workshop." Sedaris had never gone to graduate school. And although several of his stories had been photocopied, "none of them had ever been published in the traditional sense of the word" ("The Learning Curve" 83).

At first, the shaming—three insults, really—came both printed and in private.

Insult One

When students wrote to parents in jail, their work suggested what real such letters might look like. Picture two convicts—as did Sedaris—one standing at a sink while his cell mate lies reading. "Anything interesting?" the standing man asked. "Oh, it's from my daughter," the other man said. "She's just started college, and apparently her writing teacher is a real asshole" ("The Learning Curve" 88).

Insult Two

When students did "guessays" on his favorite soap, the work contained predictions like "the long-lost daughter turns out to be a vampire" and "the next day Vicki chokes to death while eating a submarine sandwich." ("Vicki" is Victoria Buchanan. The soap, *One Life to Live.*) The vampire business smacked of *Dark Shadows* reruns, and so couldn't be taken seriously. "But choking to death on a sandwich, that was an insult" ("The Learning Curve" 91).

Insult Three

When students wrote thinly veiled accounts of their own lives—Proustian or Sedaris-like stories—one man asked: "You're telling me that if I say something out loud, it's me saying it, but if I write the exact same thing on paper, it's somebody else, right?" "Yes," said Sedaris. "And we're calling that fiction." The student then pulled out a notebook, wrote something down, and handed over a sheet of paper.

"That," it read, "is the stupidest fucking thing I ever heard in my life" ("The Learning Curve" 93).

In the end, the shaming came both out loud and in public. When he handed back story evaluations, one woman—about fifteen years older than Sedaris and, to my mind if not his, Sharon-like—raised her hand:

> "Yes," she said. "If you don't mind, I have a little question." She lit a cigarette and spent a moment identifying with the smoldering match. "Who are *you*," she asked. "I mean, just who in the hell are you to tell *me* that *my* story had no ending?"

It was a worthwhile question that was bound to be raised sooner or later. Sedaris had noticed that her story ended midsentence, but that aside, who was he to offer criticism to anyone, especially in regard to writing? He'd meant to give the issue some serious thought but, between one thing and another, managed to put it out of his mind. The woman repeated the question, her voice breaking:

> "Just who . . . in the stinking hell do you think . . . you are?"
> "Can I give you an answer tomorrow?"
> "No," she barked. "I want to know now. Who do you think you are?"

Judging from their expressions, Sedaris could see that others were entertaining the same question. Doubt was spreading "like the cold germs seen in one of those slow-motion close-ups of a sneeze." And then the answer came to him:

> "Who am I?" I asked. "I am the only one who is paid to be in this room."

This was nothing to embroider on a pillow. But still, once the answer left his mouth, Sedaris embraced it as a perfectly acceptable teaching philosophy. "All right then," he added, abusively shaming—and insulting—not just that one student but the entire class: "Does anyone else have a stupid question for Mr. Sedaris?" ("The Learning Curve" 94–95, emphasis and ellipses original). ("Golly, you're a bright one, aren't you?" Lou had asked that girl. "IQ just zooming right off the charts" ["Ashes" 246]. "Smart Guy," he'd called Sedaris.) Once again, the woman raised her hand:

> "It's a personal question, I know, but exactly
> how much is the school paying you to be in this
> room?"

Sedaris answered honestly, though we're not told the amount. And then the collective laughter—both ridicule and contempt—was so loud, so violent, and so prolonged that "Mr. Sedaris" had to run and close the door so that the real teachers could do their work in peace ("The Learning Curve" 95–96).

Sedaris moved to Paris for good, but with terrible French, about ten years later. He'd tried teaching himself the language, but progress was minimal. Much as Tiffany at forty, with her *Mamma*'s and *Daddy*'s, sounded like a far-sighted baby, Sedaris at forty, in French, had only gone from speaking like an "evil baby" to speaking like a hillbilly. "Is them the thoughts of cows?" he'd ask the butcher, pointing to calves' brains. "I want me some lamb chop with handles on 'em" ("See You Again Yesterday" 164).

He'd then tried a month-long course in New York. The teacher was a nice young woman—unnamed by Sedaris. Students were to memorize simple dialogues from an audiocassette that accompanied their textbook:

Because it was a beginning course, the characters
on our tape generally steered clear of slang and
controversy. Avoiding both the past and the future,
they embraced the moment with a stoicism common
to Buddhists and recently recovered alcoholics.
Fabienne, Carmen, and Eric spent a great deal of
their time in outdoor restaurants, discussing their
love of life and enjoying colas served without ice.
Passing acquaintances were introduced at regular
intervals, and it was often noted that the sky is blue.

Once again, though, progress was minimal. Taken one
by one, the assorted nouns and verbs were within his
grasp, but due to drug use and a "close working relationship" with chemical solvents—cleaning, by that point, had
become an occupation—"it was all I could do to recite my
zip code, let alone an entire conversation devoted to the
pleasures of direct sunlight" ("The Tapeworm Is In" 182).

Sedaris then tried *Pocket Medical French,* given to
him by Amy. This phrase book and cassette, designed for
doctors and nurses unused to the language, included such
"icebreakers" as "Remove all your dentures and all of your
jewelry" (first in English, then in French) and "You now
need to deliver the afterbirth"—*Enlevez vôtre dentier et
tous vos bijoux,* and *Vous devez maintenant faire expulser
le placenta* ("The Tapeworm Is In" 185). This time, such
progress as could be made was made—probably because
he too loves shocking conversations. (Amy, looking beaten
up, had told strangers: "I'm in love. Can you believe it? I'm
finally, totally in love, and I feel great" ["A Shiner Like a
Diamond" 141].) In his case, though, such conversations
are imaginary.

Now forty-one, Sedaris took a semester-long course
in Paris. The teacher was another young woman, also
unnamed but rather mean.

Early September, First Class

Is there anyone in the room, she asked, whose first name "commences with an *ahh?*" (*Y-a-t-il quelqu'un dans la salle dont le prénom commence par la lettre A?*) Two Polish Annas raised their hands. The teacher instructed them to present themselves by stating their names, nationalities, occupations, and a brief list of things they liked and disliked. The first Anna hailed from an industrial town outside of Warsaw and had front teeth the size of tombstones. She worked as a seamstress, enjoyed quiet times with friends, and "hated the mosquito."

> "Oh, really," the teacher said. "How very interesting. I thought that everyone loved the mosquito, but here, in front of all the world, you claim to detest him. How is it that we've been blessed with someone as unique and original as you? Tell us, please."

The seamstress couldn't understand what was being said but did know this was an "occasion for shame" ("Me Talk Pretty One Day" 168). Nor, of course, could Sedaris.

Probably because he alone—clearly—cared neither for French nor about what the teacher seemed to think of his butchering it, Sedaris would receive special attention. This, however, didn't do the trick—at least not initially. As with Miss Chestnut or even "Mr. Sedaris," the shaming—insults really—came in public. And unlike the rest of the class, but like that smolderer in Chicago, he was now too old—and she too young—for "public ridicule" by the likes of her. Unlike them, moreover, he knew she was faking. No monster, no Lou at his worst, she was just an actress—like both Sharon and Amy. An actress playing the—no, not bitch. And not virago. An actress playing the "saucebox" ("Me Talk Pretty One Day" 169).

Early September, First Class: same question, *la lettre D.*

When called upon, I delivered an effortless list of things that I detest, blood sausage, intestinal pâtés, brain pudding. I'd learned these words the hard way. Having given it some thought, I then declared my love for IBM typewriters, the French word for *bruise,* and my electric floor waxer. It was a short list, but still I managed to mispronounce *IBM* and assign the wrong gender to both the floor waxer and the typewriter. The teacher's reaction led me to believe that these mistakes were capital crimes in the country of France.

"Were you always this *palicmkrexis?*" she asked. "Even a *fiuscrzsa ticiwelmun* knows that a typewriter is feminine."

Sedaris absorbed as much of this as he could understand, thinking—but, forbidden to speak English, not saying—that he found it ridiculous to assign a gender to an inanimate object "incapable of disrobing and making an occasional fool of itself" ("Me Talk Pretty One Day" 170).

Mid-September

"I hate you," she told Sedaris—in flawless English. "I really, really hate you." Call him sensitive, but he "couldn't help but take it personally" ("Me Talk Pretty One Day" 171). Stripped of the costumes and grand gestures, you recall, such acting "presents itself as an unquestionable truth" ("The Drama Bug" 105). Still, though, he *could* help but take it as an occasion for shame.

Late September

Miss Saucebox does the trick. By calling Sedaris a "lazy *kfdtinvfm,*" she finally shames him into caring what she thinks—I mean, seems to think ("Me Talk Pretty One Day" 171). Perhaps too much time had passed since the title *bum*—or even *Miss Emollient*—could either "orient" or identify him. (As children they'd "been assigned certain roles—leader, bum, troublemaker, slut—titles that effectively told us who we were" ["Repeat After Me" 144]. The Miss Emollient Pageant "was a contest judged by our mother, in which the holder of the darkest tan was awarded a crown, a sash, and a scepter" ["Genetic Engineering" 35].) Perhaps—like Proust at about the same age—Sedaris was now too old to be a slacker. At any rate, Mr. Kfdtinvfm takes to spending four hours a night on homework, putting in even more time—of course—when doing essays:

> I suppose I could have gotten by with less, but I was determined to create some sort of identity for myself: David the hard worker, David the cut-up. We'd have one of those "complete this sentence" exercises, and I'd fool with the thing for hours, invariably settling on something like "A quick run in the lake? I'd love to! Just give me a moment while I strap on my wooden leg."

Miss Saucebox, true to character, conveys "through word and action" that if this is his idea of an identity, she wants nothing to do with it ("Me Talk Pretty One Day" 171).

Mid-October

Miss Saucebox—with Amy's help—manages yet another trick by telling Sedaris, "Every day spent with you is like having a cesarean section." For the first time since moving to Paris, he understands every word someone's saying. Every medical word, at least. Of course, such understanding doesn't mean you speak the language. But its rewards are both "intoxicating and deceptive." So as the diatribe continues—"You exhaust me with your foolishness and reward my efforts with nothing but pain, do you understand me?"—Sedaris settles back to bathe in the "subtle beauty of each new curse and insult," the subtle beauty, that is, of French. "The world"—the world of Proust, in fact—has opened up. And it's with "great joy" but still terrible French that he then responds, "I know the thing that you speak exact now. Talk me more, you, plus, please, plus" ("Me Talk Pretty One Day" 172, 173).

Alisha

It takes time to learn what friends are: people who love, interest, entertain, and challenge you. People, moreover, who make you feel good about yourself. People no better or worse than you. It also takes time to learn that friends aren't selfish or competitive. We enjoy their success. (In Italian, the amiable—also undemanding—way to say *I love you* is *Ti voglio bene:* "I wish you well.") We nurture one another. And, given that friendship takes work, we aren't lazy. Attention must be paid, for however long it can. "We were friends and have become estranged," wrote Friedrich Nietzsche (1844–1900):

> But that was right, and we do not want to hide
> and obscure it from ourselves as if we had to be
> ashamed of it. We are two ships, each of which has
> its own goal and course; we may cross and have a
> feast together, as we did—and then the good ships
> lay so quietly in one harbor and in one sun that it

may have seemed as if they had already completed their course and had the same goal. But then the almighty force of our projects drove us apart once again, into different seas and sunny zones, and maybe we will never meet again—or maybe we will, but will not recognize each other: the different seas and suns have changed us! (*The Gay Science,* 159)

("What makes us unstable in our friendships," wrote La Rochefoucauld, "is that it is difficult to get to know qualities of soul but easy to see those of mind" [80].)

Sedaris at eleven promised to be his mother's friend—for a fee. Finding herself pregnant for the sixth time, with Paul, she'd had another little breakdown—not so much alcoholic, this time, as nervous. Sedaris caught her crying in the middle of the afternoon. "Are you sad because you haven't vacuumed the basement yet?" he asked. "I can do that for you if you want."

"I know you can," she said. "And I appreciate your offer. No, I'm sad because, shit, because I'm going to have a baby, but this is the last one, I swear. After this one I'll have the doctor tie my tubes and solder the knot just to make sure it'll never happen again."

Sedaris had no idea what Sharon was talking about—a tube, a knot, a soldering gun—but nodded his head as if they'd just come to an agreement:

"I can do this one more time but I'm going to need your help." She was still crying in a desperate, sloppy kind of way, but it didn't embarrass me or make me afraid. Watching her slender hands positioned like a curtain over her face, I understood that she needed more than just a volunteer maid. And, oh, I would be that person. A listener, a

financial advisor, even a friend: I swore to be all
those things and more in exchange for twenty
dollars and a written guarantee that I would
always have my own private bedroom.

"That's how devoted I was," he adds—lest we miss the self-
deprecation. But knowing what a deal this was, Sharon
dried her eyes and paid ("Chipped Beef" 6).

Between eleven and fourteen (sixth grade to ninth),
Sedaris had only one male friend. Not yet out, he hated
gay—or girlish—classmates. (See "Go Carolina" 9–11.)
Straight ones hated him, making them sexy. This, unfortunately, has been the case his entire life: "The more
someone dislikes me the more attractive he becomes"
("Full House" 37). Four such boys were Walt Winters, Dale
Gummerson, Brad Clancy, and Scott Marlboro. None of
them were popular—"they weren't good-looking enough
for that"—but each held his own on a playing field or in a
discussion about cars (32). Walt, moreover, threw rocks at
cats. Another such boy—Thad Pope—was popular and so
even sexier. Having thrown rocks at Sedaris, moreover,
Thad made him feel both particularly bad—inferior, that
is—and amiable. Even to this day, in fantasy:

> I thought about Thad a lot over the coming
> years, wondering where he went to college and if
> he joined a fraternity. The era of the Big Man on
> Campus had ended, but the rowdy houses with
> their pool tables and fake moms continued to serve
> as reunion points for the once popular, who were
> now viewed as date rapists and budding alcoholics.
> I tell myself that while his brothers drifted toward
> a confused and bitter adulthood, Thad stumbled
> into the class that changed his life. He's the poet
> laureate of Liechtenstein, the surgeon who cures
> cancer with love, the ninth-grade teacher who

insists that the world is big enough for everyone.
When moving to another city, I'm always hoping to
find him living in the apartment next door. We'll
meet in the hallway and he'll stick out his hand,
saying, "Excuse me, but don't I—*shouldn't* I know
you?" It doesn't have to happen today, but it *does*
have to happen. I've kept a space waiting for him.
("Consider the Stars" 52, emphasis original)

Dan was the exception. Ever since the fourth grade,
at nine, he and Sedaris had been "mutual outcasts—the
nature lovers, the spazzes." But things changed once Dan's
mother let him grow his hair out, at fourteen. Sharon
wouldn't allow it, perhaps because, as with earrings, she
found the combination of long hair and glasses—plus
braces—either stupid or "troubling" ("Get Your Ya-Ya's
Out!" 39). Dan "pulled ahead"—or in Nietzschean terms,
set sail. Soon his hair was "thick and straight and parted
in the middle, the honey-colored hanks pushed behind his
ears and falling to his shoulders like a set of well-hung
curtains." *Well-hung* may be otherwise indicative. Dan,
now, may have been too sexy for friendship. And besides,
he was meeting "cool" people at some new private school,
going to their homes to listen to records—becoming better than Sedaris. Guys, of course, weren't supposed to be
hurt by things like that. So instead, he settled into a
"quiet jealousy" that was very hard to hide ("The Change
in Me" 77).
    Sedaris means both jealousy and envy: jealousy in
relation to those cool people; envy in relation to Dan's
looks and status. Jealousy is vigilance in guarding a possession. Envy, as with Gretchen too about this time, is
resentful awareness of another's advantage coupled with
a desire to have it oneself. (La Rochefoucauld: "Jealousy is
in some measure just and reasonable, since it merely aims

at keeping something that belongs to us or we think belongs to us, whereas envy is a frenzy that cannot bear anything that belongs to others" [28].) Sedaris isn't vigilant about the distinction, having gotten it wrong before with Gretchen ("I had to wrestle daily with both my inadequacy and my uncontrollable jealousy" ["Twelve Moments in the Life of the Artist" 42]) but right with Sharon ("I didn't envy my mother's skill, neither did I contradict her" ["The Drama Bug" 105]).

Sedaris did have female friends. Sensing his girlishness, they found him familiar and therefore likable. Sensing their status—debased—he found them so. (Girls are to boys, within patriarchal or "heteronormative" ideologies, as gays are to straights.) There were, however, problems. Lois, at fourteen, was suddenly competitive—much like Sedaris himself. And both of them were snobs. One day, with Sedaris at the orthodontist, the *Hamlet* director— also an actor—paid their English class another visit:

> "You missed it," my friend Lois said. "The man was so indescribably powerful that I was practically crying, that's how brilliant he was." She positioned her hands as if she were supporting a tray. "I don't know what more I can say. I could try to explain his realness, but you'd never be able to understand it. Never," she repeated. "Never, never, never."

Up until then, Sedaris had never cared who made better grades or had more spending money. They each had their strengths. The important thing was to "honor" each other for whatever he did best. Lois "held her Chablis" better than Sedaris, and he respected her for that. Her "frightening excess of self-confidence" enabled her to march into school wearing a rust-colored Afro, and he stood behind her one hundred percent. She owned more records than he did, and because she was nine months older, also knew

how to drive—"as if she were rushing to put out a fire."
Fine, he'd thought. *Good for her.* His "superior wisdom and
innate generosity" had allowed him to be "truly happy"
for Lois. So who was *she*—just who in the hell was she to
question *his* intelligence? The first few visits, Lois had
been just like the rest, laughing at the guy's neck brace
and rolling her eyes at the tangerine-sized lump in his
tights. It was Sedaris who first identified his "brilliance."
And now *he'd* never understand?

> "Honestly, woman," I said to my mother on our
> way to the dry cleaner, "to think that this low-lying
> worm might speak to me of greatness as though it
> were a thing invisible to mine eyes is more than
> I can bear. Her words doth strike mine heart with
> the force of a punishing blow, leaving me both
> stunned and highly vexed, too. Hear me, though,
> for I shall bide my time, quietly, and with cunning,
> striking back at the very hour she doth least expect
> it. Such an affront shall not go unchallenged, of
> that you may rest assured, gentle lady. My
> vengeance will hold the sweet taste of the ripest
> berry, and I shall savor it slowly."

"You'll get over it," Sharon said ("The Drama Bug" 99–100,
emphasis added). But Sedaris never did avenge himself.
Nor, given how close this essay—or "project"—comes to
wounding, punishing, maybe even destroying Lois, is he
over it.

College friend Peg, unlike Lois, couldn't outpace him.
At least, not physically. She was "a fun girl with a degen-
erative nerve disease." But she, too, was a snob. Their
main fun, their only connection in fact, was fooling people.
Abusing them, in fact—though without such targets knowing. Having decided to surprise his family over break,
for example, the two hit the road—wheelchair and all.

Neither drove, of course. People would pick them up, check them into a motel, have them promise never again to hitchhike, and give money for bus fare. Sedaris would lay Peg on the bed and then sprinkle the money on her. They were pale imitations of some movie in which "crafty con artists" shower themselves with hundred-dollar bills. This version involved smaller denominations and handfuls of change, "but still, it made us feel alive." Chez Sedaris, "my brother and sisters reacted as though I had brought home a sea lion." Lou repaired the wheelchair. When Peg thanked him at dinner, he gave her another fork. "She didn't ask for a fork," said Sedaris. "She asked for your watch."

> "My watch?" he said. "The one I'm wearing?" He tapped his fingers against the face for a moment or two. "Well, golly, I guess if it means that much to her, sure, she can have my watch." He handed it over. "And your belt," I said. "She'll need that, too. Hurry up, man, the girl is crippled."

Sharon found a wad of cash for bus fare back to Ohio, then called Sedaris—alone—into the kitchen. "I don't know what kind of game you're playing," she whispered, "but you ought to be ashamed of yourself" ("The Incomplete Quad" 145, 147–49).

Peg quit that game—set sail, rather—long before Sedaris could. And the last he heard from her was in 1979, just before she died:

> Peg had undergone a religious transformation and was in the process of writing her memoirs, hoping to have them published by the same Christian press that had scored a recent hit with *Joni!,* a book detailing the life of a young quadriplegic who painted woodland creatures by holding the brush between her teeth. She sent me a three-page chapter

regarding our hitchhiking trip to North Carolina.
"God bless all those wonderful people who helped
us along the way!" she wrote. "Each and every day
I thank the Lord for their love and kindness."

This of course was sentimental and sanctimonious, as in
"Based Upon a True Story." But Sedaris—now that he, too,
knows that "people aren't foolish as much as they are
kind"—isn't being satirical at Peg's expense. At the time,
though, he wrote back saying that if she remembered
correctly, they'd made fun of people. "We lied to them and
mocked them behind their backs, and now you want
them blessed? What happened to you?" ("The Incomplete
Quad" 152).

Sedaris hooked up with another woman shortly
thereafter. This one was both able-bodied and egalitarian.
She was a reader as well:

My friend Veronica and I had been living in San
Francisco when she laid down her copy of *The
Grapes of Wrath* and announced that we'd had
enough of city living. It was her habit to speak for
the both of us, and I rarely minded as it kept me
from having to make any decisions of my own. "We
want to head up north and join our brothers and
sisters in the orchards," she said, adjusting the
scarf she'd taken to wearing on her head. "Migrant
labor, that's the life for us." The good people of this
country needed us, and we pictured ourselves
reclining in sun-dappled haystacks, eating hearty
lunches prepared by the farmer's gingham-clad
wife. ("C.O.G." 160–61)

How she'd gotten this impression from John Steinbeck was
anyone's guess, but Sedaris went along because, if nothing
else, it was guaranteed to drive Lou crazy.

They hitchhiked to Oregon, where, of course, things weren't quite as Veronica had imagined. There were no picnics in haystacks. There wasn't any gingham. The wife had cancer. And contrary to what they'd assumed, apples weren't picked off the ground but "from the limbs of hard-to-reach trees protected by a punishing bark that tended to retain a great deal of water following a good twelve-hour rain" ("C.O.G." 162). Theirs was a seven-day work-week, sunup to sundown, gentle rain or driving rain. They slept on mattresses stuffed with what Sedaris could only begin to identify as high-heeled shoes, in a cabin with no electricity and where the only source of water was a frigid, rust-caked tap. Cooking was done on a wood stove. Nonetheless, they'd return next year.

Having then found herself a boyfriend, however, Veronica backed out:

> *Boyfriend.* The word stuck in my throat like a
> wad of steel wool. "It won't last," I said. "You'll see."
> What did she need with a boyfriend? I pictured
> the two of them rolling around the floor of her
> apartment, specks of dirt being driven into their
> bare backs and pale, quivering buttocks. *Boyfriend.*
> She'd never find anyone as good as I was, I told her
> that. When she agreed, I got even angrier, storming
> off her front porch with a ridiculous, "Yeah, well,
> we'll just see about that." ("C.O.G." 162–63)

He was jealous, of course, and therefore abusive. Not to mention—having then returned alone—friendless. This was a terrible experience I'll discuss in "Martin I." For now, let me just mention that it's also one Proust had—apart from physical labor. (Proust, in fact, was rich enough never to work at all. And so the omission of any such reference with respect to Marcel is no paralipsis.) According to Walter Benjamin (1892–1940), *Remembrance of Things*

Past has isolation at its core. It's a "radical attempt at self-absorption," combining "an unparalleled intensity of conversation with an unsurpassable aloofness." (See Sedgwick 248, once again, for another view: "Is it not the mother to whom both the coming-out testament and its continued refusal to come out are addressed?" See also Genette 261: Every reader "knows himself to be the implied—and anxiously awaited—narratee of this swirling narrative.") Its "overloud and inconceivably hollow chatter," for Benjamin, is the sound of society plunging down into the abyss of loneliness. And while its ability to show things—to point a finger—is unequaled, there's another, more important gesture in togetherness or conversation: physical contact. "To no one," he writes, "is this gesture more alien than to Proust" (212).

Or at least than to Marcel. Proust's narrator is only ever touched by one friend: Marquis Robert de Saint-Loup-en-Bray, nephew to Charlus. And it happens only once. They're in a restaurant—in public, that is—at about the age of Sedaris with Veronica. To quote the entire paragraph, not—to my ear—overloud and hollow:

> After leaving us for a moment in order to
> supervise personally the barring of the door and
> the ordering of our dinner (he laid great stress on
> our choosing "butcher's meat," the fowls being
> presumably nothing to boast of) the proprietor
> came back to inform us that M. le Prince de Foix
> would esteem it a favor if M. le Marquis would
> allow him to dine at a table next to his. "But they
> are all taken," objected Robert, casting an eye over
> the tables which blocked the way to mine. "That
> doesn't matter in the least. If M. le Marquis is
> agreeable, I can easily ask these people to move
> to another table. It is always a pleasure to do

anything for M. le Marquis!" "But you must decide,"
said Saint-Loup to me. "Foix is a good fellow. I don't
know whether he'd bore you, but he's not such a
fool as most of them." I told Robert that of course I
should like to meet his friend but that now I was
dining with him for once in a way and was so happy
to be doing so, I should be just as pleased to have
him to myself. "He's got a very fine cloak, the Prince
has," the proprietor broke in upon our deliberation.
"Yes, I know," said Saint-Loup. I wanted to tell
Robert that M. de Charlus had concealed from his
sister-in-law the fact that he knew me, and ask
him what could be the reason for this, but I was
prevented from doing so by the arrival of M. de
Foix. He had come to see whether his request had
been favorably received, and we caught sight of him
standing a few feet away. Robert introduced us, but
made no secret of the fact that as we had things to
talk about he would prefer us to be left alone. The
Prince withdrew, adding to the farewell bow which
he made me a smile which, pointed at Saint-Loup,
seemed to transfer to him the responsibility for the
shortness of a meeting which the Prince himself
would have liked to see prolonged. But at that
moment Robert, apparently struck by a sudden
thought, went off with his friend after saying to me:
"Do sit down and start your dinner, I shall be back
in a moment," and vanished into the smaller room.
I was pained to hear the smart young men whom
I did not know telling the most absurd and
malicious stories about the adoptive Grand Duke
of Luxembourg (formerly Comte de Nassau) whom
I had met at Balbec and who had given me such
delicate proofs of sympathy during my grandmother's illness. According to one of these young

men, he had said to the Duchesse de Guermantes:
"I expect everyone to get up when my wife comes
in," to which the Duchess had retorted (with as
little truth, had she said any such thing, as wit, the
grandmother of the young Princess having always
been the very pink of propriety): "Get up when your
wife comes in, do they? Well, that's a change from
your grandmother—she expected the gentlemen to
lie down." Then someone alleged that, having gone
down to see his aunt the Princesse de Luxembourg
at Balbec, and put up at the Grand Hotel, he had
complained to the manager (my friend) that the
royal standard of Luxembourg was not flown in
front of the Hotel, and that this flag being less
familiar and less generally in use than the British
or Italian, it had taken him several days to procure
one, greatly to the young Grand Duke's annoyance.
I did not believe a word of this story, but made up
my mind, as soon as I went to Balbec, to question
the manager in order to satisfy myself that it was
pure invention. While waiting for Saint-Loup to
return I asked the restaurant proprietor for some
bread. "Certainly, Monsieur le Baron!" "I am not a
baron," I told him in a tone of mock sadness. "Oh,
beg pardon, Monsieur le Comte." I had no time to
lodge a second protest which would certainly have
promoted me to the rank of marquis: faithful to
his promise of an immediate return, Saint-Loup
reappeared in the doorway carrying over his arm
the thick vicuna cloak of the Prince de Foix, from
whom I guessed that he had borrowed it in order to
keep me warm. He signed for me not to get up, and
came towards me, but either my table would have
to be moved again, or I must change my seat if he
was to get to his. On entering the big room he

sprang lightly onto one of the red plush benches
which ran round its walls and on which, apart from
myself, there were sitting three or four of the young
men from the Jockey Club, friends of his, who had
not managed to find places in the other room.
Between the tables and the wall electric wires were
stretched at a certain height; without the slightest
hesitation Saint-Loup jumped nimbly over them
like a steeplechaser taking a fence; embarrassed
that it should be done wholly for my benefit and
to save me the trouble of a very minor disturbance,
I was at the same time amazed at the precision
with which my friend performed this feat of
acrobatics; and in this I was not alone; for although
they would probably have been only moderately
appreciative of a similar display on the part of a
more humbly born and less generous client, the
proprietor and his staff stood fascinated, like
race-goers in the enclosure; one underling,
apparently rooted to the ground, stood gaping
with a dish in his hand for which a party close
beside him were waiting; and when Saint-Loup,
having to get past his friends, climbed on to the
back of the bench behind them and ran along it,
balancing himself like a tight-rope walker,
discreet applause broke from the body of the
room. On coming to where I was sitting, he
checked his momentum with the precision of a
tributary chieftain before the throne of a sovereign,
and, stooping down, handed to me with an air of
courtesy and submission the vicuna cloak which a
moment later, having taken his place beside me,
without my having to make a single movement,
he arranged as a light but warm shawl about my
shoulders. (3: 561–64)

As contacts go, this of course is nurture.

Back in North Carolina, after Oregon, Sedaris discovered both conceptual art and crystal meth. ("Are you trying to punish me for something?" Sharon asked ["Twelve Moments in the Life of the Artist" 50].) He also, finally, found a group: half a dozen "brainiacs"—both women and men—who shared his taste for amphetamines and love of the word *manifesto*. Their leader's home—group headquarters—contained nothing but a giant nest of hair. It seemed he drove to all the local beauty parlors twice a week, collecting sweepings and then arranging them "as carefully as a wren" (47). Of course, being leader meant he wasn't really a friend. Nor, in fact, were the rest. Too selfish. Too high as well. So when nest builder announced plans for their next performance piece, it wasn't so much that ships set sail as that things fell apart.

Why was it always *his* piece? Who was *he* to give assignments and set deadlines? Thus questioned and also punished for having the very qualities they admired in the first place—charisma, commitment—he suggested they devise their own roles. But like Sedaris with Veronica, they all lacked the ability to think for themselves. They also resented having to admit it—unlike Sedaris back then. This, unfortunately, led to an "epic" and rather abusive shouting match in which they exhausted all their analogies and then started again from the top:

> "We're not your puppets or little trained dogs,
> willing to jump through some hoop. What, do you
> think we're puppets? Do we look like puppets to
> you? We're not puppets *or* dogs, and we're not going
> to jump through any more of your hoops, Puppet
> Master. Oh, you can train a dog. Stick your hand up
> a puppet's ass and he'll pretty much do whatever
> you want him to, but we're not playing that game

anymore, Herr Puppet Meister. We're through playing your tricks, so find someone else."

Sedaris had hoped the group might last forever, but within ten minutes "it was all over, finished, with each of us vowing to perform only our own work" ("Twelve Moments in the Life of the Artist" 50–51, emphasis added).

At some point, Sedaris did befriend other gays. Or at least one other. After Sharon died, though, he seems to have been too grief-stricken and therefore booze-dependent to sustain the relationship. Too big an asshole, as it were. I base this claim not on autobiography but autobiographical fiction. Certain truths, you recall, need masks.

"Barrel Fever"—with those "Be good" resolutions—is the fiction, Adolph Heck the mask. After his own mother's death, Adolph can't be good anymore to one Gill Pullen. Gill, too, is gay:

> I have posted some of my mother's notes on
> my refrigerator alongside a Chinese take-out menu
> and a hideously scripted sympathy card by my
> former friend, Gill Pullen. Sympathy and
> calligraphy are two things I can definitely live
> without. Gill Pullen I cannot live without. At the
> risk of appearing maudlin or sentimental it was
> mutually understood that, having enjoyed each
> other's company for seven years, we were close.
> Seeing as he was my only friend, I suppose I could
> go so far as to call him my best friend. We had our
> little fights, sure we did. We'd get on each other's
> nerves and then lay low for a couple of days until
> something good came on television, prompting one
> of us to call the other and say, "Quick—outstanding
> IV on channel seven." IV stands for innocent victim,
> usually found shivering on the sidewalk near the
> scene of a tragedy. The impact of the IV is greater

when coupled with the Wind-Blown Reporter, a
staple of every news team. Prizewinning IVs have
no notion of vanity or guile. Their presence is
pathetic in itself but that is never good enough for
the WBR, who acts as an emotional strip miner.

Gill, too, is alcoholic:

Gill was always full of good ideas. So it
shocked me when he changed so suddenly. I never
saw it coming. We made plans to meet for dinner at
an Indian restaurant that doesn't have a liquor
license. You just buy it down the block and carry it
in with you—it's cheaper that way. So Gill and I
were in the liquor store, where I asked him if we
should buy two six-packs and a pint of J&B or one
six-pack and a fifth. Or we could just go ahead and
get the two six-packs and the fifth because, why
not? I was weighing the odds when, out of nowhere,
Gill started twisting the buttons on his coat and
said, "Forget about me—you just buy something for
yourself, Dolph." Dolph is the name I go by because
really, nobody can walk around with the name
Adolph. It's poison in a name. Dolph is bad too but
it's just box-office poison.

"You go ahead, Dolph. Don't worry about me."

Later in the restaurant, figuring he'd changed
his mind, I offered Gill one of my beers. He grew
quiet for a few moments, tapping his fork against
the table before lowering his head and telling me in
fits and starts that he couldn't have anything to
drink. "I am, Jesus, Dolph, I am, you know, I'm . . .
Well, the thing is that I'm . . . I am an . . . alcoholic."

"Great," I said. "Have eight beers."

Gill became uncharacteristically dramatic,
pushing the hair off his forehead. He leaned toward

me and said, "I *can't* have a drink, Dolph. Don't you understand anything at all? I *can't.*"

He said it as though he was the recently paralyzed lead dancer in a made-for-TV movie and I had just commanded him to take the lead in tonight's production of *The Nutcracker*. I responded, acting along in what I considered an appropriate manner. "You *can* do it," I said. "I *know* you can do it. But, oh, you'd rather sit there on that chair and be a quitter. Take the easy way out. That's right— you're a loser, a cripple, but when the lights go up on that stage, when all the other dancers are in place, I want you to know the only thing keeping you in that wheelchair is yourself."

Gill's face began to buckle. When he began to sob, I realized he wasn't joking. People at the surrounding tables lowered their forks and looked over in our direction. I pointed to our plates and said in a loud whisper, "Whatever you do, don't order the tandoori chicken."

Ever since then things have been different between us. He quit calling me and whenever I called him I got his machine. His old message, the "Broadway doesn't go for pills and booze" line from *Valley of the Dolls,* had been replaced. I know he is home, screening his calls but I always hang up at the point where the new Gill's voice encourages me to take life one day at a time. What has become of him? (129–31, emphasis and ellipses original)

They seem to be in the East Village. The "box-office poison" must be Dolph Lundgren, "Ivan Drago" in *Rocky IV* (1985). And much as "what happened" to Peg was that she'd undergone a religious transformation, what became of Gill, clearly, was that he'd joined Alcoholics Anonymous

("The Incomplete Quad" 152). He'd gotten on the wagon, to use one—dual—vehicle. He'd set sail, to use another. (Metaphors consist of two parts: the tenor and vehicle. The tenor is the subject to which attributes are ascribed; the vehicle, the subject from which the attributes are borrowed. In "all the world's a stage," for example, the world is the tenor, the stage the vehicle.)

So it's no surprise that Adolph—very drunk, in some Chinese restaurant, and very jealous—then saw Gill with three other members. "Jesus," he bellowed. "Where have you been? Your parole officer has been looking everywhere for you."

Everyone in the restaurant looked up except for Gill, who shook his head and said nothing. Against my better judgment I pulled up a chair and joined their table, introducing myself as an old cellmate from Rikers Island. "Those were the days, weren't they? I think of that bunk bed every day of my life. Remember T-Bone? Remember that guy we called 'The Rectifier'? Oh, what a time!"

Nobody said anything. Gill rolled his eyes and adjusted the napkin in his lap, which, I assume, sent the "secret coded" message that I was not to be taken seriously. These were the new friends he had met at his meetings, the same type we might have made fun of a few weeks ago. Suddenly, though, they were his people.

A very thin, spent-looking woman with shoulder-length hair gathered in a ponytail cleared her throat and said, "Like I was saying earlier, I thought that Timothy person was very nice. I like him an awful lot. He's a people person, I could see that right away." This woman was missing one of her front teeth.

Another woman, younger, with heavily moussed hair fidgeted with her chopsticks and agreed, saying, "Are you talking about the Timothy with the olive-colored turtleneck and the denim jacket? Oh, I loved that guy. What a nice guy. Was he nice or what?"

"I'd say he's one of the absolute nicest guys I've met in a long time," said the sullen Abe Lincoln look-alike sitting next to me. He paused, scratching at his beard, and small stiff hairs rained onto his empty plate. "I liked Timothy right off the bat because he's just so damned nice how could you not like him?"

"Talk about nice, how about that Chip?" Gill said.

"A chip off the old block," the ugly bearded man said, at which point everyone broke into laughter.

"Ha, ha," I said. "A chip off the old shoulder."

Gill and his companions ignored me until the skinny hag turned to me and said, "You, sir, are standing in the way of our evening and I for one don't appreciate it." I suddenly understood why she was missing her front tooth.

Gill said, "Dolph, maybe you should just try to keep quiet and listen for a change." I nodded and leaned back in my chair, thinking, Listen to what? He's so nice, she's so nice, aren't they so nice. Nice is a mystery to me because while on some mundane level I aspire to it, it is the last thing I would want a table full of dullards saying about me. ("Barrel Fever" 134–37)

Niceness, after all, isn't really kindness. ("Lay some new linoleum on the floor, wouldn't that be nice?" Sedaris asked

Tiffany ["Put a Lid on It" 202].) It's both unhelpful and inauthentic. (La Rochefoucauld: "When we work for the benefit of others it would appear that our self-love is tricked by kindness and forgets itself; and yet this is the most certain way to achieve our ends, for it is lending at interest while pretending to give, in fact a way of getting everybody on our side by subtle and delicate means" [236]; "Nothing is rarer than genuine kindness; the very people who think they possess it are for the most part only easy-going or weak" [481].)

Like the relationship with Amy, the friendship with one Alisha—finally—seems trouble-free. It, too, began in childhood—we're not told when—and continues to this day. Alisha, if we're to believe the autobiography, is much kinder than Sedaris. *Sweet,* he writes, is one of her most well-worn adjectives, and she uses it to describe just about everyone. Were you to kick her in the stomach, "the most you could expect would be a demotion to 'semisweet.'" Alisha's only flaw, in fact, is that—like Sedaris under Veronica, though unlike him under the nest builder—she's "willing to do whatever anyone else wants." That, and that "like all of my friends, she's a lousy judge of character." It's hard to miss the self-deprecation there. But it's also hard, long after Sharon's death not to mention so much writing, to take it seriously ("City of Angels" 125–26).

Then again, we know only Sedaris the writer, not Sedaris the man. More on that later, in Amsterdam. For that matter, we know only Alisha the character—as she appears in "City of Angels." Unless of course, reading into Adolph's abuse, we can also—if confusedly—ascribe to her a second of Alisha's attributes. Her flaws, perhaps: formality, redundancy, officiousness, unfriendliness, and self-assertion. Until recently, we're told, Adolph had the misfortune to work at "Vincent & Skully Giftware," distributors of needlepoint beer cozies, coffee mugs in the shape of golf bags, and more insipid novelty items than you would ever want to know about:

I equate the decline of this nation with the number of citizens willing to spend money on T-shirts reading "I'm with Stupid," "Retired Prostitute," and "I won't go down in history but I will go down on your little sister." The Vincent & Skully employees were, with the exception of me, perfect reflections of the merchandise. The offices were like a national holding center for the trainably banal, occupied by people who decorated their cubicles with quilted, heart-shaped picture frames and those tiny plush bears with the fierce grip that cling to lamps and computer terminals, personalized to read "Terri's bear" or "I wuv you beary much!"

I don't know how it is that people grow to be so stupid but there is an entire nation of them right outside my door. I lost my job a few months ago when Alisha Cottingham went off the deep end and cornered me in the mailroom. Alisha is in the marketing division and she tends to use what she considers to be concise, formal speech. Listening to her speak I imagine she must type it up the night before and commit it to memory, pacing back and forth in her godforsaken apartment and working to place the perfect emphasis on this or that word.

"Mr. Heck," she began, blocking me off at the Xerox machine. "It has come to my attention here at V&S Giftware that you seem to have some problem with my chin. Now, let me tell you a little something, sir. I am not here to live up to your stringent physical qualifications. I am here to work, as are you. If my chin is, for any reason, keeping you from performing your job here at Vincent & Skully then I believe we have a problem."

What chin? Adolph had said something about this Alisha's neck. Her chins were another story.

> She continued. "I just want you to know that your deliberate cruelty cannot hurt me, Mr. Heck, because I will not allow it to. As a professional I am paid to rise above the thoughtless, petty remarks of an office boy who takes his pleasure in remarking upon the physical characteristics of his coworkers, many of whom have fought valiantly against both personal and social hardships to make this a company we can all be proud of." Eventually she began to sob and I might have felt sorry for her had she not reported me twice for smoking dope during the three o'clock break. So I made some little remark and it got around. So what? Did Alisha Cottingham honestly believe that by sitting beside me and sharing a bag of potato chips our bond would grow so strong I would fail to notice she has a neck like a stack of dimes?

There seemed no stopping her. Alisha Cottingham would finish her speech then start all over again from the top, each delivery louder than the last, until the manager arrived. Maybe, the man suggested, you'd be happier somewhere else. "Happier?" Adolph now responds ("Barrel Fever" 133–34).

Vincent Skully, by the way, was an art historian at Yale—which neither Adolph nor Sedaris attended. And like Skully, Adolph—clearly—was a snob. Like Veronica, though, Gill may not have been.

Martin I

One's employer—much like that nest builder—isn't one's friend. He's more like a parent or teacher. As such, he can be abusive. This Sedaris learned relatively young.

He and Dan—that one male friend—had shared an occasional job at Dorton Arena, a concert hall on the North Carolina state fairgrounds. When lucky, they worked the concession stand. When unlucky, they worked the aisles, hawking popcorn, peanuts, and "ice-cold" soda. That description came from a boss who, to Sedaris, seemed like a redneck. To the boss, customers did:

> In real life nobody said things like "ice-cold drinks," but our boss, Jerry, insisted on it. Worse than simply saying it, we had to shout it, which made me feel like a peddler or an old-time paperboy. During heavy-metal concerts we went unnoticed, but at the country-music shows— jamborees, they were called—people tended to

complain when we barked through their favorite songs. "Stand by Your POPCORN, PEANUTS, ICE-COLD DRINKS," "My Woman, My Woman, My POPCORN, PEANUTS, ICE-COLD DRINKS!" "Folsom Prison POPCORN, PEANUTS, ICE-COLD DRINKS." The angrier fans stormed downstairs to take it up with Jerry, who said, "Tough tittie. I got a business to run." He dismissed the complainers as "a bunch of tightwadded rednecks," which surprised me, as he was something of a redneck himself. The expression *tightwadded* was a pretty good indicator, as was his crew cut and the asthma inhaler he'd decorated with a tiny American flag.

"Maybe he means 'redneck' in an affectionate way," Sharon said. Far more likely, Jerry saw a difference between himself and the people who looked and acted just like him. Sedaris did this too, of course, and listening to Jerry made him realize how "pathetic" it sounded. "Who was I to call someone uncool—me with the braces and thick black-framed glasses" ("The Change in Me" 75–76).

When the fair opened, the two worked both the arena and a nearby speedway. Walking from one to the other, moreover, they soon learned a second trade. They learned— by example—how to beg:

> It was the easiest thing in the world. Dan worked one side of the Ferris wheel, and I took the other. We asked for money the way you might ask for the time, and when someone gave it we blessed them with a peace sign or the squinty nod that translated to, "I'm glad you know where I'm coming from."

This, they felt, was freedom. It was delinquency as well. And so one day, they reached the speedway to find Jerry alone setting up for a stock-car race. "I ought to kick ya'll's asses," he said. "Walking out on me the way you done, that's no way to treat a friend." Didn't do the trick. Sedaris and Dan then announced both having found an easier way to make a living and their decision to quit. "Then get on out of here. And don't come crawling back, neither. I don't have no use for backstabbers" ("The Change in Me" 79–80).

The man for whom Sedaris picked apples in Oregon— at first with Veronica, the next year by himself—seemed like a bumpkin. (The two had hitchhiked from California. Sedaris, alone, took the bus from North Carolina.) Like that eighth-grade Spanish teacher, he was racist as well. "Whole-aah, Toe-moss," he shouted while leading Sedaris— without Veronica—by the barn where one dark-eyed man stood waiting to shower. "Hola, Señor Hobbs." "You speak some Mexican, don't you Daniel?" Hobbs asked Sedaris. "Well, by God, I'm learning a few words of my own. A person *has to* in order to get along in the modern world!" Times have changed, he explained as they continued the tour. Kids around here—slackers—think they're too good to work. Only choice left is either trash or Mexicans, and he'll take the stupid Mexicans any day. "Watch this," he said: "Bueños Dios, Miguel." Another such man looked up from his wood splitting, alarmed. "They spook easy," Hobbs further explained. Well, Sedaris thought, people do that when you sneak up behind them yelling *Good God!* ("C.O.G." 164, emphasis original).

He then worked at a packing plant. Management there, Sedaris imagined, would be exploitative. Sedaris himself would rabble-rouse—would lead, in fact:

> The plant was located between town and
> [Hobbs's] farm. A corrugated, ramshackle eyesore
> of a building, it housed an archaic network of
> shuddering conveyor belts that moved as if they

were powered by a team of squirrels running a treadmill somewhere in the basement. Nothing about the place was inviting, but I suspected that might change the moment they handed me my union card. I would soon be a Teamster, a title guaranteed to cost my father a good three nights' sleep and to drive my former friends wild with envy. In time, everyone would be affected. Looking out upon the busy plant floor, I imagined all these people seated in folding chairs as I addressed them from the stage of the meeting hall. "Brothers and sisters," I would yell, clutching a bullhorn in one callused hand and a stack of documents in the other, "the time to act is *now!* They call this a contract? Well, I call it a *contrast,* the difference between the way things *are* and the way things *ought to be!*" I would need to pause here, as the applause would be deafening. "It's *us,* the working people of this country, who make the world go round, and until management opens their eyes to that fact, until the fat daddies upstairs are ready to park their Cadillacs and negotiate a decent wage, *this* is what I have to say to their contract."

Fellow Teamsters would "stand on their seats and cheer" as Sedaris ripped the contract into pieces and tossed it over his shoulder ("C.O.G." 168, emphasis original).

Sedaris, of course, did nothing of the sort. Nor was management exploitative. Due to harassment by a "brother" named Curly, however, Sedaris decided not only to quit but to leave town immediately. (Curly, to my mind if not that of Sedaris, functions like Charlus at Balbec.) So he turned in some library books—presumably the ones that helped distinguish what he did enjoy from what he thought he should—and then stopped by both to announce

and to explain that decision. "Yale," he shouted to the fore-
man over the noise of a generator. "I have to head back
East because they want me to teach at Yale."

> "You what?" he shouted. "Who's going to jail?"
> "No, YALE."
> "All right then, just make sure you don't bend
> over to pick any soap off the shower floor. We'll see
> you when you get out." ("C.O.G." 179–80, emphasis
> original)

> Before leaving, though, Sedaris worked for the
> next-to-last stranger from whom I imagine he'd
> ever accept a ride.

Jon Combs, although born-again, was neither sentimental
nor sanctimonious. He was, however, both abusive and
selfish—unlike the family who, out of both love and pity,
had loaned him their basement. (Jon made clocks down
there. Cases, rather—from jade shaped to resemble Oregon. Sedaris, using scraps, would make boxes too—stash
boxes.) Jon belonged to their church. And having lost one
leg in an accident and then the other to gangrene, he had
artificial legs.

It was Jon's habit to begin each day with a prayer.
But was he the only person in the room? "My pal Jesus
is looking down here saying, 'I know that's Jon, but who's
that puddin'head with the stupid smirk on his face?' Hurry
up now, get down on that floor and act grateful you've got
the knees to bend on." When Sedaris assumed the position, Jon would say:

> "Hi there, Lord. It's me again, your old buddy Jon.
> If it's not too much to ask, I'd like you to keep an
> eye on this disrespectful mutt I've got working for
> me. Let me be patient and try my best to teach him
> about you and this precious jade you've given me.

And hey, thanks for the coffee, but do you have any sugar? HA!"

"You can joke with the Lord," he explained. "Hey, up there. I sure hope nobody takes me to court. I wouldn't have a leg to stand on. HA!" ("C.O.G." 184).

The charm of such instruction faded once they set to work. Jon would use a pressurized saw to cut jade into quarter-inch-thick slices. These Sedaris then sanded, using a variety of graded discs that fit upon a rapidly spinning wheel. Once smooth, he'd polish the slices against a rotating belt. As the friction generated heat, he'd occasionally drop a piece, sending it shattering onto the floor. "You stupid, clumsy jackass," Jon would shout, pounding his canes against the table. "Do you know how much work went into that? You goddamned silly mutt!" Having exhausted Sedaris, he'd then appeal to heaven:

"Hey, Lord, why are you treating me this way?
Is this some kind of a test? Did you send me this
butterfingered fuckup in order to teach me a
lesson? What did I do to deserve this stinking shit?"

At this point, the door leading to the basement would open, and a woman would poke her head over the banister. "Brother Jon, is there a problem?"

"Oh, I've got a problem all right. This son of a bitch just dropped four hours' worth of backbreaking work on the fucking floor. *That's* my goddamned problem."

"I'm very sorry to hear that," the woman would say, covering the ears of her five-year-old daughter ("C.O.G." 185, emphasis original).

Because born-again, Jon was homophobic as well. This Sedaris learned the morning after his own tearful, short-lived, and isolation-based conversion:

I was a Christian now, a Christian. Hopefully I
could skip the phase of wearing large crosses and
handing out pamphlets titled *The Devil in Mr.
Jones* or *Satan's Slaughterhouse*. Bypassing the
hopelessly corny sing-alongs and church-basement
potluck suppers, I intended to move straight into
a position of judgment. People would pay me to
tell them what they were doing wrong, and in
criticizing their every move, I would aid all
mankind. With any luck I could do this without
having to read the Bible or eat anything containing
marshmallows.

This—judge people—Sedaris now tries *not* to do. (But Jon
is judged, as was Lois.) He does, however, try to help us.
At any rate, he began his new life both by telling Jon his
real reason for quitting the plant and by coming out of
the closet: "So, he took me into his bedroom and it turned
out . . ."

"That guy was a homo, right?" Jon curled his
lips in disgust. "That happened to me once back in
the army. There's a lot of sick people in this world.
The guy asked if he could hold me, that's what he
said. 'Can I hold you?' I still had legs then and I
used them to kick his ass. But you're that way, too,
aren't you?"

I nodded my head.

"I knew it the first time I saw you operate a
sander. I said, 'That guy is sick.' And you are, aren't
you? You're sick."

He said it with concern, the way you might
address a friend with tubes running from his nose.
"You're sick." I attempted to re-create my crying
jag, but it sounded false. "Boo-hoo-hoo. Aww-ha-ha-
hu-hu-hu-hu." There was no mucus, and I had to

provoke my eyes with my fingers to produce tears. "A-he-he-hu-hu-hu."

"Don't cry to me. Tell it to Jesus," Jon said. "Reach out to him. Tell him you're sorry. Crouch down there on the floor and pray, for God's sake."

"Oh, God, hu-hu-hu, I'm so sorry I met that guy. He was so stupid."

"And tell Him you're never going to do it again," Jon shouted.

"And I'll never do it again," I said. "No Curly, never again."

"With any man. Tell Him you're never going to lay down with any other man. Tell Him you want to get married."

"Oh, please," I said. "Please let me get married."

"To a woman," Jon said. "Married to a woman."

"Toman," I said, hoping that if the transcript were ever brought to heaven's court, I could not be accused of making promises I didn't keep. "Toman." Somewhere along the line, I had forgotten this might be part of the deal. Couldn't you be the type of Christian who judged people *and* slept with guys?

"And tell Him you're sorry for taking long lunches and being so clumsy," Jon added ("C.O.G." 194–95, emphasis and ellipsis original).

Eventually, though, he dropped the concern. Driving Sedaris back from a crafts fair at which the boxes sold but clocks didn't, Jon exploded:

"Let me tell you a little something. I don't appreciate being used. I'm not talking here about all the free coffee and rides I've given you. I mean used in here." He meant to point at his heart but, swerving to pass another car, wound up gesturing toward his lap instead. "You're a user, kid. You used

my tools and my patience and now you want me to
pat you on the head and tell you what a good little
boy you are. But you know what? You're *not* a good
boy. You're not even a good girl."

Anger, of course, along with envy, are sins—which of course
didn't occur to Jon. The diatribe continued:

"You wear me out with your sob stories and then
expect me to dust you off and tell you Daddy's
going to make everything all right. But you know
something, kid? I'm *not* your daddy and I'm tired of
being used like one."

And then Sedaris got fired—for the very first time. (The
next time, when Lou kicked him out, resulted from homophobia alone: "I felt as though he were firing me from the
job of being his son" ["Hejira" 87].) Worse yet, Jon did it
abusively: pulling off the highway, telling Sedaris, "I'm not
your daddy *or* your chauffeur *or* your goddamned Santa
Claus," kicking him out, and then taking off. Sedaris, to
his credit, "blessed" the rear end of the moving car with a
rock. Well, he thought, it wasn't too far back to his trailer
at the farm. No more than ten miles. So Sedaris walked a
ways. But—having realized that "if I hurried, I could clean
the place up and get my things together in time to catch
the morning bus home"—he then held out his thumb
("C.O.G." 200–201, emphasis original).

Now, it's possible that Sedaris, with a father like
Lou, was looking for a daddy. ("Until the fat daddies
upstairs are ready to park their Cadillacs and negotiate a
decent wage," he'd imagined telling Teamsters, "*this* is
what I have to say to their contract" ["C.O.G." 168, emphasis original].) Tiffany was. It's also possible he still is. But
I doubt "Brother Jon" fit the bill. Nor did "brother" Curly,
as you'll see in a bit. For one thing—like both Sedaris and,

according to Sharon, Lou—Curly's a mama's boy. ("It's fat, my ass," she'd told him, "but not as big as the can on that prize heifer you've got shoveling down three sacks of clover she harvested from the Kazmerzacks' front yard, mama's boy" ["Get Your Ya-Ya's Out!" 32].)

At any rate, once back in North Carolina, Sedaris did maintenance work at apartments both Lou and Sharon owned. Lou, of course, was abusive, with most of the abuse stemming from how cheap—or *tightwadded*—he was. He also, if inadvertently, used shame to nurture:

> On a selfish note, "The Empire," as we liked to call it, provided me with an occasional job—a week of painting or weatherproofing or digging up a yard in search of a pipe. The downside was that I'd be doing these things for my father, meaning that the pay was negotiable. I'd present a time card, and he would dispute it, whittling my hours to a figure he considered more reasonable. "You expect me to believe you were there every day from nine to five? No lunch, no cigarette breaks, no sitting in the closet with your finger up your nose?"

A "video monitor in my head" would show Sedaris engaging in these very activities, he now admits. Lou, somehow, would catch a glimpse of it. "I knew it," he'd say. "I'll pay you for thirty hours, and that's just because I'm nice" ("Slumus Lordicus" 93).

Sedaris did similar work in Chicago, for an anti-Semite. "Let's see," Uta said upon entering an apartment the two of them—with assistance—would renovate. "What sort of mess did our little Jewess leave behind?" ("Something for Everyone" 212). You buy a building, she explained, but your hands are tied until old tenants leave. Lucky for her, their fat little Jewess was the first to go—a short little thing with an ass the size of a beanbag chair. And

Christ Almighty, was she ever a slob. Jews, you see, were a thorn in Uta's side. Something about Hitler being completely misunderstood. Something about a conspiracy between the Jews and Stalin, who for various reasons had set their sights on her native Lithuania. The communists wanted the country in order to enslave the hardworking population; the Jews, for forests they'd use as toilet paper. So Uta despised them, also blaming Jews for everything from the high cost of cable to traffic jams.

Sedaris, as an employee, was in no position to argue. Nor was coworker Dupont—about whom, more later. But Polly could. Polly was a benevolent friend of Uta's who'd arrive to help—no charge—and also, having finally snapped, to both shame and out her. One day, when Polly complained of having gotten bad seats at a Cubs game, Uta explained that all the good ones were taken by the Jews, who also controlled the hot dog concessions and souvenir sales. The parking, the players' salaries, even the making of bats and mitts, it was all controlled by the Jews. And they've been shooting the prices right through the roof. Here she was, two blocks from Wrigley Field, and they're driving her property taxes sky-high. "Aw, shut up, already," Polly interrupted:

> "You've been carping about the Jews ever since you
> left that dump of a country. Open up a third-grade
> history book and maybe you'd learn something.
> Besides, you didn't think the Jews were so bad back
> when you were chasing Brandy Fleischman."

That did the trick—and probably *because* done in public. Or at least, in front of people over whom, as an employer, Uta had authority. (That's why shaming teachers immediately, even—or especially—by their students, might work.) People, that is, from whom—like Jon—she wanted respect. ("If it's not too much to ask," he'd prayed, "I'd like you to

keep an eye on this disrespectful mutt" ["C.O.G." 184].)
Uta blushed. She huffed. She fidgeted. She brushed her
bangs back from her forehead the way she had a thousand
times before, "but now the gesture was openly nervous."
Then she pulled the hair back over her eyes as if to hide
herself and, after a long, uncomfortable pause, muttered,
"Well, Brandy was only *half* Jewish." "Yeah?" Polly asked.
"Which half, top or bottom?" Sounds, to me, like Sharon
("Something for Everyone" 228, emphasis original).

Sedaris worked for another cheapskate in New York:
an heiress who, more as a hobby than as a moneymaker,
ran a publishing company out of a town house and who,
although rich, preferred to pretend otherwise. Having paid
for the house in cash, for example, Valencia furnished it
with broken tables and chairs she'd picked up off the street.
So in addition to filling a few orders, copying a few letters,
and making some phone calls, Sedaris would spend most
of his time mentally redecorating. Worse yet, she haggled
over everything. If some cabdriver charged four dollars,
"she'd wrangle him down to three." If some cash-strapped
merchant or laborer demanded the previously agreed-upon
price, she'd accuse him of "trying to fleece a poor immigrant
woman with a small, struggling business and a child to
feed." Worn out by such "bickering"—which is to say, such
lying, manipulation, and *shameless* use of shame—many of
them caved. This, of course, Sedaris found awful. He was
surprised as well by the "joy" Valencia took in saving money
she didn't need, at other people's expense. Once again,
though, he was in no position to argue. Nor, as her sole
employee, was he himself positioned to shame—not even
when, half his paychecks having bounced, she refused to
reimburse him for penalty charges. It was his bank's fault,
she claimed, not hers ("The Great Leap Forward" 102–3).

The next and last employer, still in New York, was as
nonabusive—as egalitarian, in fact—as possible. Patrick

did control the means of production, a moving van. As a communist, however, he hated for Sedaris—or any employee—to consider him the boss. "This is a collective," he'd tell them. "Sure, I might happen to own the truck, but that doesn't make me any more valuable than the next guy. If I'm better than you, it's only because I'm Irish." Now, Sedaris hadn't liked any self-proclaimed Marxist back in college. Patrick, though, was different. "One look at his teeth, and you could understand his crusade for universal health care." That is, like his glasses, they were held together with duct tape. Notable too was his willingness to do physical labor—unlike those Marxists, who'd believed that come the revolution, "they'd be the ones lying around party headquarters with clipboards in their hands." (Think D. A. Miller.) So Sedaris both loved the job, moving furniture, and considered Patrick not the boss, but "my friend the communist" ("The Great Leap Forward" 109, 114).

Still, though, Patrick *was* the boss. "My friend the communist" could only have been meant with both fondness and irony. Should he alone have wanted something done, or not done—so be it. Sometimes they'd walk into an organized, well-packed apartment, and if the client was male and clearly successful, Patrick would cancel, claiming that his axle had broken or the truck's transmission had given out. "Sorry, friend," he'd say, "but I just can't do it." He'd give the guy some competitor's number and then—much like Valencia fleecing a merchant—leave "delighted by the great inconvenience he'd caused."

> "Guys like that are bad news," he'd say,
> heading back to the truck. "So how about it, boys,
> are any of you up for a piping hot cup of coffee?
> My treat."
> I was rarely appeased by the words *piping hot*.
> I didn't want a cup of coffee, I wanted to work.

"What was wrong with that guy?" I'd ask. "It was an elevator building, for God's sake. That was money."

Patrick would throw back his head and let out his hearty communist laugh, an extended bray that suggested I was young and could not tell the difference between good money and bad.

"We'll do a big job tomorrow," he'd say. "Relax, brother. How much money do you need?"

"Enough for a town house," I'd say. ("The Great Leap Forward" 117)

In other words: what's the difference, really, between Jerry's "ice-cold," back in Raleigh, and Patrick's "piping hot"? Come to think of it, maybe "brother" Patrick was, if not the kind of daddy Sedaris—mistakenly—had imagined at the plant, then the kind Brother Jon—correctly—had imagined he himself was not.

Most coworkers aren't friends, either. Rather, they don't become friends. For every Dan selling ice-cold drinks or Veronica picking apples, there are many more Adolph Hecks dismissing Alisha Cottinghams as both "banal" and "stupid" or Alisha Cottinghams inadvertently getting them fired ("Barrel Fever" 133). This, too, Sedaris learned young. At sixteen, he dismissed those cafeteria workers as both ignorant and lazy:

Like several of the other local cafeterias, the Piccadilly often hired former convicts whose jobs were arranged through parole officers and work-release programs. During my downtime I often hung around their area of the kitchen, hoping that in listening to these felons, something profound might reveal itself. "It suddenly occurred to me that we are all held captive in that prison

known as the human mind," I would muse, or "It
suddenly occurred to me that freedom was perhaps
the greatest gift of all." I'd hoped to crack these
people like nuts, sifting through their brains and
coming away with the lessons garnered by a
lifetime of regret. Unfortunately, having spent the
better part of their lives behind bars, the men and
women I worked with seemed to have learned
nothing except how to get out of doing their jobs.
("Dinah, the Christmas Whore" 108)

Those apple pickers, in turn, dismissed Sedaris—now
without Veronica—as both needy and talkative:

During the first few weeks, Hobbs would
turn off his tractor and we'd talk for a while before
he carried off the bin. Once he realized how much
I had to talk about, he took to leaving the motor
running. "Gotta go check on the wife," he'd shout.
"You keep up the good work." The Mexicans were
now jogging past my trailer on their way to the
shower.

Then all but one of the apple packers, whom Sedaris considered "the little people," dismissed him as both boastful
and snobbish ("C.O.G." 166, 169). The exception was Curly.

During his first hour at the plant, Sedaris had made
the mistake of trying an apple. "Fresh from its chemical
bath, it burned my lips and the flesh at the corners of
my mouth, leaving a harsh aftertaste that lingered long
after I'd run to the bathroom and washed my mouth out
with soap." During their break one evening, he asked if
any of his female coworkers happened to speak Italian.
"I studied it for a year back in college," he said. "And now
I've completely forgotten the word for 'tragedy.' Oh, I know
Spanish, too, and a wee bit of Greek, but Italian is so, well,

bellissimo, isn't it?" Such attempts to impress—if not to lead—failed miserably. The women took to calling Sedaris *Einstein.* "I could tell you were a smart one the first time I saw you bite into one of those apples," one brayed. "I said to myself, now *there's* someone with a good head on his shoulders." The room filled with laughter. "Hey, Einstein," asked another, "what's the Latin word for 'blowhard'?" ("C.O.G." 169, 171, emphasis original). Such Sharon-like behavior, on their part, combined teasing, shaming, and insulting.

Curly—whom Sedaris considered a "loser"—did offer friendship. But of course he had sex in mind. This finally became clear to Sedaris when, three weeks into the job, he joined Curly—and his mother—in their own trailer for a drink:

> "Mother? Are you decent? The number-one
> son is home." He opened a door at the end of the
> hallway, and I saw a thin, shriveled stalk of a
> woman lift herself from the toilet. I turned my head
> then, pretending to examine a picture of a spry
> granddad, spreading his arms wide to indicate the
> length of the one that got away.
>   "I thought you were one of those Taylor boys,"
> the woman said. "I thought you were coming for
> that big crate of franks. Their father dropped them
> off, a whole big crate of them. I called and said,
> 'I don't know what a person would do with so many
> franks. Send your boy out after them.'"
>   Curly lowered his voice. I could not catch the
> words, but the tone was one of impatience.
>   "No, sir, I do not want you to get the stick,"
> I heard the woman say. "I want those wienies out of
> my closet is what I want. Call that Taylor boy on
> the phone and see if he can't come get them."

I heard her protest as she was lifted, heard
the toilet flush and the sound of water running in
the sink. "I don't have the buns for franks like that.
Call them up and see won't they come."

Curly opened the door and emerged with his mother in
tow, leading her past the kitchen and into a room Sedaris
knew he didn't want to enter. This was one of those times
he literally kicked himself for never having learned to
drive. With his own car, he could have made up some
excuse and cleared out with no problem. He could have
taken Curly's car if only he knew how to drive it:

"Boy, is she tired or what?" Curly said,
shaking his head in disbelief as he left the
bedroom. "Sometimes she's just like a clock, if you
know what I mean. Cuckoo. Cuckoo." He rotated
his index finger against the side of his head. "You
know how it is with mothers. Can't live with them,
can't fit them into a burlap sack. Hey, did I say
that?" He pressed a finger to the tip of his nose as
if it were a button labeled REWIND. "Did we come
here to relax or what?" He stepped into the kitchen
and returned with a six-pack of beer, explaining
that we should probably retire to his bedroom, as
his mother was a light sleeper. "She can be, oh
boy, a regular three-headed monster when she
doesn't get her shut-eye," he said. "You're not like
that, are you? Are you a cranky old werewolf when
you wake up in the morning? I sure hope not,
because I'm askaird of monsters." He chewed his
nails and buckled his trembling knees. "I'm askaird.
I'm afwaid."

It gets even worse and, for writing by Sedaris, rather
graphic. In the end, he claimed to have crabs. Curly claimed

not to mind. ("Come on now, get your ass in this bed. Curly will find those mean old crabs and spank the shit out of them.") And then Sedaris did clear out—on foot ("C.O.G." 174, 175–77, 178).

Back in Raleigh, apart from working for Lou, Sedaris cleaned construction sites. His coworker there—much like both Sedaris and Curly at the packing plant—was an alleged genius unhappy with the course his life had taken. ("You and me are a lot alike," Curly had said. "I'm probably a good fifteen years older and nowhere near as smart as yourself, but come January I'm enrolling in a management class over at the community college" ["C.O.G." 172].) He'd always talk about how smart he was, and it was always the same conversation:

> "Here I am with a one-thirty IQ, and they've got me sweeping up sawdust." He'd glare at the bristles on his broom as if they had conspired to hold him back. "Can you beat that? A one-thirty! I'm serious, man. I've been tested."
>
> This was my cue to act impressed, but I generally passed.
>
> "One three oh," he'd say. "In case you didn't know it, that's genius level. With a mind like mine, I could be *doing* something, you know what I mean?"
>
> "Absolutely."
>
> "Pulling nails out of two by fours is not what I was made for."
>
> "I hear you."
>
> "A sixty could do what I'm doing. That leaves me with extra IQ points sitting around in my head doing nothing."
>
> "They must be bored."
>
> "You're damn right they are," he'd say. "People like me need to be challenged."

"Maybe you could turn on the fan and sweep against the wind," I'd suggest. "That's pretty difficult."

"Don't make fun of me. I'm a lot smarter than you."

"How do you know?" I'd ask. "I might be a three hundred or something."

"A three hundred. Right. There's no such thing as a three hundred. I'd place you at around seventy-two, tops."

"What does that mean?" I'd ask.

"It means I hope you like pushing a broom."

"And what does *that* mean?"

He'd shake his head in pity. "Ask me in about fifteen years."

Fifteen years later Sedaris found himself working—in New York—for a housecleaning company. Yes, it was unskilled labor, but for what it's worth, he did very little sweeping. Mainly he vacuumed. And when several years after that— in Paris—Sedaris himself took the test, he turned out "really stupid, practically an idiot." But we're not told the score ("Smart Guy" 239–40, 246, emphasis original).

Some of the work Sedaris did for that cleaning company was with a presumably white man. All we really know is that he wasn't a friend. They were cleaning the apartment of a *Sesame Street* writer when Sedaris grabbed one of her eight Emmy Awards off the window ledge and, "posing before a full-length mirror, looking humble," delivered a well-rehearsed acceptance speech:

"I really wasn't prepared for this," I said, hoping the audience might believe me. I have spent the better part of my life planning my awards speeches and always begin with that line. It is tiresome to listen as winners thank people most of

us have never heard of, but in my award fantasies
I like to mention everyone from my twelfth-grade
English teacher to the Korean market where I buy
my cigarettes and cat food. And that's what's nice
about eight Emmys. Lifting each one I addressed
the mirror, saying, "But most of all I'd like to thank
Amy, Lisa, Gretchen, Paul, Sharon, Lou, and Tiffany
for their support." Then I picked up the next,
moving on to Hugh, Evelyne, Ira, Susan, Jim,
Ronnie, Marge, and Steve.

By the eighth Emmy, he was groping, trying to recall the
name of some camp counselor. Enter Bart, whom only now
did Sedaris—"with shame"—realize he hadn't thanked.
To add to the shame, perhaps, posing before that mirror
couldn't possibly have involved *really* looking at himself—
as Sharon had suggested. But at least—"hoping the audience might believe me"—Sedaris was more or less self-
conscious about it. And at least he had many more friends
by then than he seems to have had at the time of her
death: Hugh, Evelyne, Ira, Susan, Jim, Ronnie, Marge, and
Steve. Hugh must be Hugh Hamrick, about whom, more
later. Ira, I imagine, is the public radio producer Ira Glass
("The Curly Kind" 165–66).

Dupont, the black man with whom Sedaris had
worked under Uta, was insufficiently authentic—and far
too duplicitous—to be a friend. The duplicity consisted of
his actually trying to get Sedaris fired. (It didn't happen.
At least, not that way.) The inauthenticity—like that of
Sedaris himself at the plant ("I know Spanish, too, and a
wee bit of Greek" ["C.O.G." 171]) but unlike that of Valencia—consisted of his pretending to be whomever he thought
you might expect. To an anti-Semitic and therefore racist
landlady, for example, he played the "grinning minstrel."
To what he considered a sex-crazed homosexual, he was

the "indefatigable stud." (Who then, wondered Sedaris, "was he to his mother?") Friends, of course, do entertain one another. And much of this was entertaining—only not the way Dupont had intended. Sedaris, that is, "enjoyed" his stories, but only, in part, because he never quite believed them. It wasn't, say, the seventh-grade math teacher measuring Dupont's erect penis with a slide rule or even his claim to have "poured motor oil on a college girl's titties" that captivated Sedaris, "rather it was the notion that he thought I might be impressed" ("Something for Everyone" 219–20).

Under Patrick, Sedaris worked with Lyle, a guitar-playing folksinger from Queens; Ivan, a Russian immigrant on medication for what had been diagnosed as residual schizophrenia; and Richie, "who, at six feet four and close to 350 pounds, was a poster boy for both the moving industry and the failure of the criminal rehabilitation system." Convicted at fifteen, Richie had served ten years in a combination of juvenile and adult penitentiaries on charges of arson and second-degree murder. The victim had been his sister's boyfriend, whom he'd burned to death because, "I don't know—the guy was an asshole." This he then retracted:

> "Rather, I found him to be untrustworthy. How's that?" In an effort to impress his latest parole officer, Richie was trying to improve his vocabulary. "I can't promise I'll never kill anyone again," he once said, strapping a refrigerator to his back. "It's unrealistic to live your life within such strict parameters."

And just as Sedaris ironized Patrick as "my friend the communist," implying thereby that they couldn't be that close, he does the same for Ivan and Richie: "my friend the schizophrenic," and "my friend the murderer." Lyle, for some reason, gets no such epithet ("The Great Leap Forward" 110–11, 114).

As "Crumpet," a thirty-three-year-old elf in Macy's SantaLand, Sedaris at first dismissed both himself and anyone else wearing such a costume as a "poor, pathetic, son of a bitch." He then realized how deliberately entertaining—and perhaps impressive—many of them are. There's Puff, from Brooklyn:

> We were standing near the Lollipop Forest when we realized that *Santa* is an anagram of *Satan.* Father Christmas and the Devil—so close and yet so far. We imagined a SatanLand where visitors would wade through steaming pools of human blood and feces before arriving at the Gates of Hell, where a hideous imp in a singed velvet costume would take them by the hand and lead them to Satan.

There's Sleighbell, who's been on television:

> I asked if she has ever done *One Life to Live,* and she said, yes, she had a bit part as a flamenco dancer a few years ago when Cord and Tina remarried and traveled to Madrid for their honeymoon.

There's Snowball, who hams it up with children—"sometimes literally tumbling down the path to Santa's house."

> I tend to frown on that sort of behavior but Snowball is hands down adorable—you want to put him in your pocket. Yesterday we worked together as Santa Elves and I became excited when he started saying things like, "I'd follow *you* to Santa's house any day, Crumpet."

It made Sedaris dizzy, this flirtation. By midafternoon he was running into walls. At the end of their shift, however, they were in the bathroom, changing clothes, "when suddenly we were surrounded by three Santas and five other elves—all of them were guys that Snowball had been flirting with." Maybe some of them—the Santas, at any rate—were daddies as well ("SantaLand Diaries" 168, 180, 181–82, 184, emphasis original).

Of course, these elves—and Santas—are entertaining not because they're friends let alone boyfriends of Sedaris, but because they're entertainers. Like Sleighbell on *One Life to Live* or Sedaris himself in *Hamlet*—nowadays at readings, on recordings, on the radio, or even just in print—most of them in real life are show business people. (Proust, by all accounts, was not one.) Here at Macy's, moreover, they still are. *All* of them, that is, including Sedaris. (Recall Sharon's having encouraged him to perform.) They're all performing theatrical roles for customers, for themselves, and for one another as well: the generic role of "elf," of course; but beyond that, such individual ones—derived in part from assigned roles like leader, bum, troublemaker, and slut—as Crumpet, Puff, Sleighbell, and Snowball. Like Sedaris alone before that mirror, moreover, they're doing so self-consciously. Unlike him—now they've got an actual audience, several in fact (coworkers, parents, children)—they're doing so ironically. They're both wearing masks—or costumes—and indicating them, though not of course to children. They're both associating themselves with and dissociating from impersonations. Except, that is, for both "Santa Santa," who won't reveal his real name, and—if only at the very end—Crumpet. Call it method acting—like Amy on *Strangers with Candy,* or telling strangers she's in love. Or method working. Call it, perhaps, *elf*-consciousness.

It's Christmas Eve, the last day of work—but also "a day of nonstop action." Managers have been spending a lot of time with walkie-talkies. Parents in long lines have been leaving diapers at the door to Santa's house. One father called Santa a faggot because he couldn't take the time to recite "The Night before Christmas." One mother "experienced a severe, crowd-related anxiety attack: falling to the floor and groping for breath, her arms moving as though she were fighting off bats." Two others got into a fistfight. It was, in sum, "the rowdiest crowd I have ever seen." Plus they were "short on elves," many of whom simply didn't show up or called in sick. So lunch hour was cut in half, and breaks eliminated. Elves who had shown up complained bitterly, of course. Not Crumpet, though. "It was time to be a trouper," the essay nearly concludes, "and I surrendered completely" ("SantaLand Diaries" 196).

A career as part-time slacker, part-time author began at this point. (The first radio broadcast had been in 1992. The first collection—*Barrel Fever*—appeared in 1994.) Because both writing and cleaning left Sedaris pretty much on his own, he no longer had coworkers to contend with—aside from Bart. Nor—ignoring editors or producers—did he have employers. The sole exception: the man for whom they did that Emmy winner's apartment:

> My boss ran a small agency and charged fifteen dollars an hour, five of which went to him and ten to the employee. You could earn more working for yourself, but to me it was worth it to have a middleman, someone to set up the schedule and take the occasional flak. If something was broken, our boss would replace it, and if something was stolen, or alleged to have been stolen, it was he who defended our character. With the exception of a chiropractor's office, all of my jobs were residential, apartments and lofts I visited once a week or once every other week. The owners were usually off at

work, and on the few occasions that they were home they tried to make themselves as unobtrusive as possible. ("Blood Work" 123–24)

Sedaris did, however, now have his own customers: both readers (or listeners) and residents over whom, on occasion, he could exercise authority and from whom, like Uta, he probably wanted respect. Readers and residents, that is, whom Sedaris could shame in pretty much the same way—as a nurturer—but with rather different results. As a writer, I imagine, the shamings usually did the trick. As a cleaner, the only one we're told of did not.

Such shaming didn't come out of nowhere. Sharon, of course, had set a great example. But for customer relations in particular, there was daddylike Patrick telling that yuppie—in not so many words—to take his job and shove it. Best of all, there was Lena—not so lazy after all:

My housecleaning role model was a woman named Lena Payne, who worked for my family in the late 1960s. I used to come home from school and watch with great interest as she tackled the kitchen floor. "Use a mop," my mother would say, "that's what I do," and Lena would lower her head in pity. She knew what my mother did not: either you want a clean floor or you want to use a mop, but you can't have both. Whether it was ironing or deciding how to punish a child, Lena knew best, and so she became indispensable. Like her, I wanted to control households and make people feel lazy and spoiled without ever coming out and saying so. "Didn't you have potato chips *yesterday?*" she'd ask, frowning at the can as big as a kettle-drum my sisters and I parked in front of the TV. Suggesting that potato chips were an overindulged luxury caused them to lose their taste and meant there'd be fewer crumbs to vacuum at the end of the day. She was smart, and very good at her job. I worshipped her. ("Blood Work" 132, emphasis original)

For Marcel, the Lena figure had been Françoise:

I should not myself have felt that Mme de Guermantes was irritated at meeting me day after day, had I not learned it indirectly by reading it on the face, stiff with coldness, disapproval and pity, which Françoise wore when she was helping me to get ready for these morning walks. The moment I asked her for my outdoor things I felt a contrary wind arise in her worn and shrunken features. I made no attempt to win her confidence, for I knew that I should not succeed. She had a power, the nature of which I have never been able to fathom, for at once becoming aware of anything unpleasant that might happen to my parents and myself. Perhaps it was not a supernatural power, but could have been explained by sources of information that were peculiar to herself: as it may happen that the news which often reaches a savage tribe several days before the post has brought it to the European colony has really been transmitted to them not by telepathy but from hill-top to hill-top by beacon flares. Thus, in the particular instance of my morning walks, possibly Mme de Guermantes's servants had heard their mistress say how tired she was of running into me every day without fail wherever she went, and had repeated her remarks to Françoise. My parents might, it is true, have attached some servant other than Françoise to my person, but I should have been no better off.

Françoise was in a sense less of a servant than the
others. In her way of feeling things, of being kind
and compassionate, harsh and disdainful, shrewd
and narrow-minded, of combining a white skin
with red hands, she was still the village girl whose
parents had had "a place of their own" but having
come to grief had been obliged to put her into
service. Her presence in our household was the
country air, the social life of a farm of fifty years
ago transported into our midst by a sort of holiday
journey in reverse whereby it is the countryside
that comes to visit the traveler. As the glass cases
in a local museum are filled with specimens of the
curious handiwork which the peasants still carve or
embroider in certain parts of the country, so our flat
in Paris was decorated with the words of Françoise,
inspired by a traditional and local sentiment and
governed by extremely ancient laws. And she
could trace her way back as though by clues of
colored thread to the birds and cherry trees of her
childhood, to the bed in which her mother had died,
and which she still saw. But in spite of all this
wealth of background, once she had come to Paris
and had entered our service she had acquired—
as, *a fortiori,* anyone else would have done in her
place—the ideas, the system of interpretation used
by the servants on the other floors, compensating
for the respect which she was obliged to show to us
by repeating the rude words that the cook on the
fourth floor had used to her mistress, with a servile
gratification so intense that, for the first time in
our lives, feeling a sort of solidarity with the
detestable occupant of the fourth floor flat, we said
to ourselves that possibly we too were employers
after all. This alteration in Françoise's character

was perhaps inevitable. Certain ways of life are so
abnormal that they are bound to produce certain
characteristic faults; such was the life led by the
King at Versailles among his courtiers, a life as
strange as that of a Pharaoh or a Doge—and, far
more even than his, the life of his courtiers. The
life led by servants is probably of an even more
monstrous abnormality, which only its familiarity
can prevent us from seeing. But it was actually in
details more intimate still that I should have been
obliged, even if I had dismissed Françoise, to keep
the same servant. For various others were to enter
my service in the years to come; already endowed
with the defects common to all servants, they
underwent nevertheless a rapid transformation
with me. As the laws of attack govern those of
riposte, in order not to be worsted by the asperities
of my character, all of them effected in their own an
identical withdrawal, always at the same point, and
to make up for this took advantage of the gaps in
my line to thrust out advanced posts. Of these gaps
I knew nothing, any more than of the salients to
which they gave rise, precisely because they were
gaps. But my servants, by gradually becoming
spoiled, taught me of their existence. It was from
the defects which they invariably acquired that I
learned what were my own natural and invariable
shortcomings; their character offered me a sort of
negative of my own. We had always laughed, my
mother and I, at Mme Sazerat, who used, in
speaking of servants, to say "that race," "that
species." But I am bound to admit that what made
it useless to think of replacing Françoise by anyone
else was that her successor would inevitably have
belonged just as much to the race of servants in

general and to the class of my servants in
particular. (3: 76–79)

Françoise, of course, lived in. Lena did not.

As a *negative* role model—an abusive shamer—there
was, of course, Lou. But for customer relations, once again,
there was Jerry telling those rednecks, "Tough tittie. I got
a business to run" ("The Change in Me" 76). Best of all,
there was the manager with whom "SantaLand Diaries"
actually concludes:

> It was time to be a trouper, and I surrendered
> completely. My Santa and I had them on the lap,
> off the lap in forty-five seconds flat. We were an
> efficient machine surrounded by chaos. Quitting
> time came and went for the both of us and we paid
> it no mind. My plane was due to leave at eight
> o'clock, and I stayed until the last moment, figuring
> the time it would take to get to the airport. It was
> with reservation that I reported to the manager,
> telling her I had to leave. She was at a cash
> register, screaming at a customer. She was, in fact,
> calling this customer a bitch. I touched her arm and
> said, "I have to go now." She laid her hand on my
> shoulder, squeezing it gently, and continued her
> conversation, saying, "Don't tell the store president
> I called you a bitch. Tell him I called you a fucking
> bitch, because that's exactly what you are. Now get
> out of my sight before I do something we both
> regret." (196)

Not virago—"bitch."

Sedaris himself, however, had some practice even
before New York. Back in Chicago, of course, there'd been
that writing workshop. Students, after all, are like customers. Many, unfortunately, even think of themselves as

such. Then there was physical labor to be done—supposedly. Sedaris, miserable, had been perusing his school's employment notebook:

> Page by page it mocked my newly acquired
> diploma. Most of the listings called for someone
> who could paint a mural or enamel a map of
> Normandy onto a medallion the size of a quarter.
> I had no business applying for any of these jobs or
> even attending the Art Institute in the first place,
> but that's the beauty of an art school: as long as
> you can pay the tuition, they will never, even in the
> gentlest way, suggest that you have no talent.

In other words, shame on them. Suddenly, though, Sedaris came across the number of a woman who wanted her apartment painted. He had plenty of experience there. If anything, he was considered too meticulous a painter. So as long as she supplied the ladder and he could carry the paint on the bus, "I figured I was set" ("Something for Everyone" 204).

Sedaris telephoned. The woman began by saying she'd always painted the apartment herself:

> "But I'm old now. It hurts my hands to massage
> my husband's feet, let alone lift a heavy brush over
> my head. Yes, sir, I'm old. Withered and weak as a
> kitten. I'm an old, old woman." She spoke as if this
> were something that had come upon her with no
> prior notice. "All the sudden my back gives out, I'm
> short of breath, and some days I can't see more
> than two feet in front of my face."

This was sounding better all the time—and even better than work for Valencia, with all that mental redecorating, would turn out to be. Sedaris had learned to be wary of people forced to pay others for jobs they used to do themselves. "As a rule they tended to be hypercritical." But with her, he didn't think there would be a problem. "It sounded as if she couldn't see anything well enough to complain about it." He could probably just open the paint can, broadcast the fumes, and call it a day—lazy bastard. Anyway, they made arrangements for him to visit the following morning ("Something for Everyone" 204–5).

The apartment was on Lake Shore Drive. The door was answered by a trim, energetic woman holding a tennis racket. Her hair was white, but her skin smooth and unwrinkled. Sedaris asked to speak to this woman's mother, and she chuckled, poking him in the ribs with the racket handle:

> "Oh, I am just so happy to see a young person." She grabbed my hand. "Look what we've got here, Abe: a young fella. Why, he's practically a toddler!"
>
> Her husband bounded into the room. Muscular and tanned, he wore a nylon fitness suit complete with a headband and sparkling sneakers. "Ahh, a youngster."
>
> "He's a graduate," the woman said, squatting to perform a knee bend. "A kid, thinks he's ready to paint our sarcophagus. He's looking at us thinking he's discovered a pair of fossils he can maybe sell to a museum. Oh, we're old all right. Out to pasture. Long in the tooth."
>
> "Built the pyramids with my own hands," the husband added. "Used to swap ideas with Plato and ride a chariot through the cobbled streets of Rome."
>
> "Face it, baby," his wife said. "We're ancient. A couple of has-beens."

This routine—this entertainment, really—went on and on. And every time Sedaris tried to turn the subject to the work at hand—to painting—they wouldn't hear of it:

"Stay for lunch, why don't you," the woman said. "I'll just hook Old Crusty up to his feeding tubes and throw us together a couple of sandwiches."

"A sandwich!" the man cried. "How are you planning to manage the bread? Those chops of yours can't take on anything harder than applesauce."

"Well, I can still chew *you* out!" she said. "And they don't come any harder than that." ("Something for Everyone" 205, 207, emphasis original)

Sedaris drew up an estimate and phoned the next day, knowing it might be a waste of time. It was:

"Listen, doll, it seems we've decided not to have the place painted after all. Not much point in it, seeing as we'll probably be packed off to the nursing home before you get your ladder set up."

It was his role—his assigned role—to contradict the woman. Instead, Sedaris tried shaming her. "You're probably right," he said. "As feebleminded as you are, I guess it's about time to make plans for a structured environment." But it didn't do the trick. Too insulting, probably. Too abusive. "Hey now," she said, shaming him—immediately—in return. "No need to get ugly" ("Something for Everyone" 207).

Nor, when working for that cleaning company, did Sedaris get to shame the first New Yorker he mentions having been home—a rather shameless asshole who should have been unobtrusive. As with Mrs. Crusty, Sedaris only got to *be* shamed:

This afternoon I went to G.L.'s apartment to clean his venetian blinds, which had been soiled during a fire. I first met this man last week when I

was sent to unpack his books and arrange them
on the shelves in alphabetical order. He's got quite
a library: leather-bound editions of Jane Austen
and Émile Zola sandwiching several cookbooks
and countless manuals devoted to the study of
sadomasochistic sex. This morning G.L. answered
the door in his bathrobe, drinking black coffee
from a mug shaped to resemble a boot. He is not a
pleasant man but seems to get along fine in the
world as long as he has his way. He led me to the
nearest window and suggested I use Formula 409
and paper towels, but that would have taken me
weeks. Having experience with blinds I thought it
might be quicker and more productive if I took
them down and washed them in the tub. I thought
he would argue with me but instead he took off his
bathrobe saying, "Sure, whatever." He stood for a
moment in his underpants before walking into the
bathroom, where he ran water into the sink,
preparing to shave something. G.L.'s bathroom is
tiny and I thought he might need some privacy, so
I just sort of stood around the living room until he
called out, "Hey, are you going to clean those blinds
or not? I'm not made of money."

I took down one of the blinds, slowly and
carefully, as if I were removing a tumor from a
sensitive area of the brain. I stood with the blinds
in my hands and counted to twenty. Then to thirty.
He called out again and I had no choice but to
press against him as I entered the bathroom.
I passed him at the sink and made my way to the
tub, where I knelt down and commenced to bathe
the venetian blinds in water and ammonia. G.L.
had a television propped beside the sink, a portable
TV the size of a car battery, which he would

constantly curse and rechannel. I couldn't see the
screen but listened as he groused his way from one
Saturday-afternoon program to another before
settling on an infomercial devoted to something
called "The Oxygen Cocktail." From what I could
hear I gathered that The Oxygen Cocktail is some
sort of pick-me-up made from clarified air. The
commercial suggested that early cavemen enjoyed
a highly satisfying oxygen content, which afforded
them the stamina to produce magnificent cave
paintings and still find the energy to hunt
mastodons. Participants in the recent Olympic
Games testified to the virtues of The Oxygen
Cocktail, and I listened while bending over the
bathtub, scrubbing a sadist's blinds with ammonia.
I wanted to part the shower curtain, curious to see
this Oxygen Cocktail. Does it come in a can, a
bottle, a nasal spray? Were the Olympians in
swimsuits or street clothes?

    The blinds weren't coming clean the way
I'd hoped so I added some Clorox to the mixture, a
stupid thing to do. The combination of ammonia
and chloride can be lethal but I've discovered it can
work miracles as long as you keep telling yourself,
"I want to live, I want to live. . . ." I tried reminding
myself of that fact. I pictured myself finishing the
job and returning home to a refreshing Oxygen
Cocktail. My throat began to burn and I heard G.L.
begin to buckle and cough. When he parted the
curtain asking, "Are you trying to kill me?" I had to
think hard for the answer. ("The Curly Kind"
163–65, ellipsis original)

As for that library ("leather-bound editions of Jane Austen"), I'm reminded of what Leo Bersani once wrote:

The macho-style for gay men . . . gives rise to two
reactions, both of which indicate a profound respect
for machismo itself. One is the classic put-down:
the butch number swaggering into a bar in a
leather get-up opens his mouth and sounds like
pansy, takes you home, where the first thing you
notice is the complete works of Austen, gets you
into bed, and—well, you know the rest. In short
the mockery of gay machismo is almost exclusively
an internal affair, and it is based on the dark
suspicion that you may not be getting the real
article. The other reaction is, quite simply, sexual
excitement. (208)

In other words, some daddy. But I'm also reminded of what
D. A. Miller writes about this "ferocious" impersonation by
Bersani:

Even to its own sense of itself, the joke couldn't be
more banal. Yet could it ever be too "tired," as we
say, to *work*, to elicit automatically, from virtually
any audience, the knowing laugh of folkloric
literacy? On the contrary, the synergy of stereo-
types motors an irresistible force in which no
sooner has the Woman been announced in the
drawing room than, with duly inopportune
eagerness, the Woman Inside charges out of the
closet to rejoin her. And so continues into sexual
maturity, even by his own kind, the shaming of the
boy Austen reader, who seems (if we might keep up
the shaming a bit longer) to have learned so little
from past experience, to have amassed so meager a
store of pop culture capital, that his childhood
indiscretion is likely to go on being repeated till
the end of his clueless days. As compulsively as
the author of a "perfect crime" is undone by his

unconscious need to get its perfection recognized,
this incurable queen can't help laying his closet
open to the view it was built to obstruct. (*Jane
Austen*, 4–5, emphasis original)

As usual, Miller's also really talking about Proust. He and
Bersani, by the way, were coworkers—colleagues, rather—
at the same university.

The second such New Yorker asked Sedaris to do
something shameful—a request that involved not the
man's being an asshole but his having one. Sedaris had
been cleaning this apartment for over a year before they
ever met. A claims adjuster in his mid-sixties, the man
was home recovering from an operation. Something about
heart trouble. "I hate to bother you," he said, "but I'm
going to lie down for a while. I've set the alarm, but if
for some reason I don't wake up, I'm wondering if you
could possibly insert this into my anus." He then handed
Sedaris a rubber glove and a suppository.

"If you're not awake by when?" I asked.
"Oh, say, three o'clock."

Sedaris wondered what to do if the alarm didn't wake him.
"Which was worse—inserting a lozenge into a stranger's
anus or feeling responsible when his heart stopped beating?" As with most things, it depended on the person. The
man had never complained or asked Sedaris to do laun-
dry. He'd been thoughtful enough to supply a glove. "So
who was I to deny him this one favor?" The alarm rang.
But just as Sedaris was screwing up his courage, the man
emerged from his bedroom, "looking refreshed and ready
to take on the afternoon." He returned to work the following week. And so they never saw each other again. The boss,
not surprisingly, was horrified to learn all this. Sedaris,
however, now sees it not as another missed opportunity to

shame a customer—immediately—but as an "adventure" ("Blood Work" 124, 125).

A third such opportunity presented itself with the boss on summer vacation. No middleman. Once again, though, Sedaris failed to do the trick—as far as we know. Not by abusing the customer, as with Mrs. Crusty. And not by taking abuse, as with that leather queen. ("Hey, are you going to clean those blinds or not?" ["The Curly Kind" 164].) Sedaris failed, this time, because he hadn't *been* a trick.

After reading a *New York Times* article titled "He Does Radio *and* Windows," a shameless—no, not asshole—diabetic named Martin wrote *David Sedaris* on a piece of paper and then looked him up in the phone book. Confusingly enough, the paper also contained the name and number of an erotic cleaning service he'd read about in a porn magazine. So Martin called Sedaris, mistaking him for "the sexpot" ("Blood Work" 135). And Sedaris accepted what he mistook for an ordinary job.

The apartment was located in the East Eighties. The door was answered by a man "in his mid-forties, plump, with a round, sunburned face and damp, wheat-colored hair" ("Blood Work" 126). The air conditioning was off. And Martin, to put it mildly, was obtrusive. He'd follow Sedaris from room to room. He'd hint Sedaris should take off his clothes. Sedaris preferred not to. He'd ask loaded questions about Fire Island. Sedaris pretended not to get them. Through it all, moreover, Sedaris would remain truly oblivious. Even the possibility of mistaken identity wouldn't occur to him until just after Martin took matters into his own hands—or hand—and then paid, and paid, and paid.

Sedaris began with the kitchen. When finished there, he did the bedroom. When finished there, he moved on to the living room—Martin, as usual, toddling two steps behind. Sedaris gathered some newspapers and magazines

into a pile. Then he dusted the TV. Martin sank onto the
sofa and activated a tape in the VCR. It was a military
story. Some private had failed to shine the sergeant's
boots, and now there would be hell to pay. "You ever seen
this?" Martin asked. Standing there, sweat dripping off
his face, Sedaris wondered how Lena might have reacted
"had one of us peeled off our pants and proceeded to masturbate to a movie called *Fort Dicks.*" (Think Mireille
Dujardin.) They didn't have video back then, but if they
had, he surmised, she'd probably say what Sedaris did: "I
don't have a VCR." (What this meant was: "Your behavior
troubles me," or *Shame on you.*) And then he turned away
("Blood Work" 132–33, 135).

But it was Sedaris who felt ashamed:

> *Whack, whack, whack. Whack, whack, whack.*
> Martin's forearm batted against a newspaper lying
> at his side, and I turned on the vacuum in order to
> cover the noise. There was no way I was going to
> acknowledge either him or the TV, and so I kept my
> head down, reworking the same spot until my
> shoulder started to ache and I switched arms. *Just
> pretend it isn't happening,* I told myself, but this
> was unlike ignoring a subway car musician or a
> crazy stranger seated next to you at a restaurant
> counter. Like the cough of a sick person, Martin's
> efforts broadcast germs, a debilitating shame bug
> that traveled across the room in search of a new
> host. How terrible it is to be wrong, to go out on a
> limb and make an advance that isn't reciprocated.
> I thought of the topless stay-at-home wife, opening
> the door to the gay UPS driver, of all those articles
> suggesting you surprise that certain someone by
> serving dessert in the nude or offering up an
> unexpected striptease. They never tell you what to

do should that someone walk out of the room or look at you with that mix of disgust and pity that ten, twenty, fifty years later will still cause you to burn every time you think about it. I've had some experience in this department, and Martin's depressing, wrongheaded display brought it all flooding back. I thought of the time . . . And of the time . . .

He doesn't, however, appear to have thought of Curly. At any rate: "*Whack, whack, whack. Whack, whack, whack.*"

It had now become the kind of masturbation that's an extended exercise in determination rather than pleasure. You'd give up but, godammit, you're the kind of person who carries a job through to the end, whether it's making a fool of yourself in front of a stranger or vacuuming somebody's living room. *I will finish this,* you think. *I will finish this.* And he did, eventually climaxing with a bleak, long-winded moan. The paper at his elbow ceased its rattling, the video was off, and after pulling up his pants, he scooted into the bedroom. I didn't expect him to come back out and was surprised when he returned moments later with a stack of cash.

Twenty, forty, sixty, eighty. Martin counted softly, and with a different voice than had been used for the past two hours. This one was higher and passive, shaded with the kind of relief that follows a "prolonged impersonation." *A hundred and ten, a hundred and twenty.* Martin stopped at two hundred, more than six times what Sedaris should have made, and then added a thirty-dollar tip. "Is that right?" he asked ("Blood Work" 133–34, ellipses original).

"Let me ask you something," Sedaris responded. End of story, more or less. Essay, rather. But then, I imagine, Martin's own shame began.

Martin II

Sedaris tends to satirize strangers. We're either foolish or vicious. He tends to stereotype as well. Dupont, for example, is either Grinning Minstrel or Indefatigable Stud. So it takes both time and effort for Sedaris to see us as individuals—no worse but also no better than himself, not to mention no less complicated. (La Rochefoucauld: "It is easier to know man in general than to understand one man in particular" [436].) It takes further time and effort to realize that some of us, in turn, stereotype and perhaps satirize Sedaris. This jibes with Proust, where no characters—except, of course, the narrator—turn out to be as heterosexual, or even as malevolent, as they seem. Or—like Dupont—as they pretend. Charlus, for example, or the unnamed friend of Mlle Vinteuil.

   He and Peg—in college—enjoyed dismissing people who'd given them rides as fools. Most of them, in fact, were kind. On his own, though, such drivers were unkind: older men not only wanting sex—like Charlus—but demanding

it. Older men, moreover, who—like T.W.—might even kill
Sedaris:

> I was looking out at the road and didn't see
> it coming. He grabbed me by the hair and yanked
> my head down onto the seat, holding me there
> with one hand while he reached into his jacket
> pocket with the other. The truck swerved and
> skidded onto the gravel shoulder before he took
> the wheel and regained control. There was
> something cold and blunt pressed hard against
> my jaw, and even before I saw it clearly, I
> understood it was a gun. Its physical presence
> inspired an urgency lacking in any of the movies
> or television dramas in which it plays such a key
> role. "You like that, do you?"

These, he felt, were "professional maniacs" ("Planet of the
Apes" 136).

After college, Sedaris dismissed fellow bus passengers
as either "motor-mouthed simpletons" or "shiftless idiots."
Curly dismissed coworkers as "morons." Sedaris disagreed.
But then Curly got him promoted over women with senior-
ity. The women, understandably enough, accused Sedaris
of having "slept his way to the middle." "Next thing you
know," one whispered, "he'll be wearing fur-lined gloves
with a cushion propped under his little fanny." She must
mean Sedaris, the only one there with that size ass. And so
Curly was right. These women *were* morons. *Slept his way
to the middle.* Did they honestly think he'd been asleep?
Of course, as may have become clear to him once Curly,
too, demanded sex—"Come on now," he'd said, "get your
ass in this bed"—the real moron was Sedaris ("C.O.G."
155, 159, 172, 173, 178).

In New York, one experience taught Sedaris to continue being dismissive. Alisha, visiting from North Carolina,

had made the mistake of bringing some "monster." Bonnie—the monster—was cheap:

> She showed me the taxi receipt, and I assured
> her that this was indeed the correct price. It was a
> standard thirty-dollar fare from Kennedy Airport
> to any destination in Manhattan.
>
> She stuffed the receipt back into her wallet.
> "Well, I hope he wasn't expecting a tip, because he
> didn't get a dime out of me."
>
> "You didn't tip him?"
>
> "Hell no!" Bonnie said. "I don't know about
> you, but I work hard for my money. It's mine and
> I'm not tipping anybody unless they give me the
> kind of service I expect."
>
> "Fine," I said. "But what kind of service did
> you expect if you've never ridden in a cab
> before?"
>
> "I expect to be treated like everybody else is
> what I expect. I expect to be treated like an
> American."

She was selfish:

> I've had visitors from all over, but Alisha's
> friend was the first to arrive with an itinerary, a
> thick bundle of brochures and schedules she kept
> in a nylon pack strapped around her waist. Before
> leaving North Carolina, she'd spoken with a travel
> agent who'd provided her with a list of destinations
> anyone in her right mind would know to avoid,
> especially around the holidays, when the crowds
> multiply to Chinese proportions.
>
> "Well," I said, "we'll see what we can do. I'm
> sure Alisha has places she'd like to go, too, so
> maybe we can just take turns."

The expression on her face suggested that give-and-take was a new and unpleasant concept to Bonnie of Greensboro. Her jaw tightened, and she turned back to her brochures, muttering, "I came to New York to see New York and isn't nobody going to stop me."

And she was abusive:

Our troubles began the following morning when I disregarded the itinerary and took the two women to the Chelsea flea market. Alisha wanted to look for records and autographs. Bonnie wasn't much of a shopper, but after a pronounced bout of whining, she decided she wouldn't mind adding to her lifelong angel collection. Angels, she said, were God's way of saying howdy.

The flea market was good for records and autographs, but none of the angels mustered an appropriate howdy. "Not at these prices. I asked some lady how much she wanted for a little glass angel playing a trumpet, and when she said it cost forty-five dollars, I told her to go straight to you know where. I said there's no way I'm paying that much when back home I can get ten angels for half that price. 'And,' I said, 'they'd be a lot more spiritual than the sorry-looking New York angels y'all have here.' That's exactly what I told her."

She pronounced the flea market a complete waste of time, adding that she was cold and hungry and ready to leave. It was decided that even though $1.50 was a lot to charge for a ten-minute ride, we would take the subway uptown and get something to eat. Things went smoothly until the transit clerk accidentally shorted her a nickel and Bonnie stuck her mouth into the token window, shouting, "Excuse

me, but for your information, I do not appreciate
being taken for a fool. I may be from Greensboro,
North Carolina, but I can count just as well as
anyone else. Now, are you going to give me my five
cents, or should I talk to your supervisor?"

Sounds, to me, like Lou. To Bonnie, though, Sedaris was
"Mr. New York City" ("City of Angels" 127–29, 130).

Another experience taught Sedaris to stop being dismissive. Too lazy to diet or exercise, he decided that a
week in a nudist colony might help him feel less ashamed
of his body—of his now not so little ass in particular. He
might even lose weight:

> Last night I was in a foul mood and provoked
> Hugh into a fight, goading him until he left the
> bedroom, shouting, "You're a big, fat, hairy pig!"
>
> *Big* is something I can live with. *Fat* is open
> to interpretation, but when coupled with the word
> *hairy,* it begins to form a mental picture that is
> brought into sharp focus when united with the
> word *pig.* A big, fat, hairy pig. Well, I thought, pigs
> provide us with bacon and watchbands, and that's
> saying something. Were they able to press buttons
> and operate levers with their sharp hooves, they
> would have been sent into space long before
> monkeys. Being a pig isn't so bad. I wiped a driblet
> of snot from the tip of my snout and lay there
> feeling sorry for myself. If I were a nudist, Hugh's
> words wouldn't have hurt me, as I would have
> accepted myself for who I am. There were, of course,
> other options. I could trot down to the local
> gymnasium and tone myself up. It's a nice word,
> *gymnasium,* unfortunately it's also archaic. Gone
> are the jump ropes and medicine balls of my youth.
> Now there are only health clubs and one-syllable

gyms where sweat-drenched he-men bulk up through the use of weight machines and Stair-Masters. I've seen them through the front windows of the city's many fitness centers. Dressed in costumes as tight as sausage casings, these men and women intimidate me with their youth and discipline. It's them who have removed both the *g* and the *h* from the word *light,* reducing it to its current, slender version. Everything is "lite" now, from mayonnaise to potato chips, and the word itself is always printed in bright colors so your eyes won't get fat while reading the label. Diet and exercise are out of the question as far as I'm concerned. My only problem with nudism is that I don't even walk around my house barefoot, let alone naked. It's been years since I've taken off my shirt at the beach or removed so much as my belt in the presence of strangers. While I long to *see* naked people, I'm not so sure I'm ready to be naked myself. Perhaps the anxiety will cause me to drop a few pounds and I'll come out a double winner. The less I have to accept of myself, the easier it will be. Already I can feel my appetite waning. ("Naked" 253–54, emphasis original)

About that provocation, more later.

Having just taken a cab from the bus station, Sedaris dismissed fellow colonists as "freaks" ("Naked" 252, 274). This was because seeing their naked bodies—in public—*defamiliarized* or *estranged* them. (Defamiliarization is a concept developed by the Russian formalists Boris Eichenbaum and Viktor Shklovsky; estrangement, by the German playwright Bertolt Brecht [1898–1956].) It's also because he didn't see them naked. He saw them *nude*. "To be *naked* is to be oneself," writes John Berger:

To be *nude* is to be seen naked by others and yet
not recognized for oneself. A naked body has to be
seen as an object in order to become a nude. (The
sight of it as an object stimulates the use of it as an
object.) Nakedness reveals itself. Nudity is placed
on display. (54)

After a few days, though, Sedaris accepted the colonists
as ordinary. This was because—as with those "brainiacs"
doing both conceptual art and crystal meth—he'd joined
the group. "Suddenly it felt normal to tuck my cigarettes
into my socks and head out the door carrying nothing but
a towel." It's also because he got to know them:

There was with Roberta, and with everyone
I'd met, something larger and more definitive than
her nudity. People were stamp collectors and
gardeners, ham radio operators, registered nurses,
and big-time pet owners. It was no different than
anywhere else, except that while describing their
passions, these people just happened to be naked.
("Naked" 285, 288)

Sedaris, here, gets Berger's distinction right. As with envy
and jealousy, though, he was wrong before. You "long to
see" not naked but nude people (254).

By week's end, estrangement worked backwards.
Sedaris, self-consciously clothed, was now back at the station. There were college students in baggy, knee-length
shorts, bank tellers in navy blue suits. Other people had
stockings. Others, handbags:

Bodies, fat and thin, were packed into slacks
and pleated skirts. Every outfit resembled a
costume designed to reveal the aspirations of the
wearer. The young man on the curb would like to
make the first Olympic skateboarding team. The

girl in the plastic skirt longs to live in a larger
town. I found myself looking at these people and
thinking, *I know what you look like naked. I can
tell by your ankles and the tightness of your belt.
The flush of your face, the hair sprouting from your
collar, the way your shirts hang off those bony hips:
you can't hide it from me.* ("Naked" 290)

And so the naked body now symbolized, for Sedaris, people as we really are: not just without clothes but without
"costumes." People, that is, beyond stereotype. Beyond
professions like registered nurse, bank teller, or, for that
matter, maniac. Beyond passions like stamp collecting,
skateboarding, or, for that matter, exercise. And so, perhaps, beyond satire.

Both in and out of Paris—with Hugh or without—
several experiences taught Sedaris that some see him both
stereotypically and satirically. Spending time on the subway, he finds Bonnie aboard. Or rather, Carol and Martin—
no relation to the diabetic:

Hugh and I boarded our second train, where
an American couple in their late forties stood
hugging the floor-to-ceiling support pole. There's no
sign saying so, but such poles are not considered
private. They're put there for everyone's use. You
don't treat it like a fireman's pole; rather, you grasp
it with one hand and stand back at a respectable
distance. It's not all that difficult to figure out,
even if you come from a town without any public
transportation.

The train left the station. Needing something to hold on to,
Sedaris wedged his hand between the couple and grabbed
the pole at waist level. The man turned to the woman, saying, "Peeeeew, can you smell that? That is pure French,

baby." He then removed one of his hands from the pole and waved it in front of his face. "Yes indeed," he said. "This little froggy is ripe." It took a moment to realize he was talking about Sedaris.

> The woman wrinkled her nose. "Golly Pete!" she said. "Do they all smell this bad?"
> "It's pretty typical," the man said. "I'm willing to bet that our little friend here hasn't had a bath in a good two weeks. I mean, Jesus Christ, someone should hang a deodorizer around this guy's neck."
> The woman laughed, saying, "You crack me up, Martin. I swear you do."

It's a common mistake, writes Sedaris, for vacationing Americans to assume that everyone around them is French and therefore speaks no English whatsoever. These two didn't seem especially mean. And back home they probably would have had the "decency" to whisper. Here, however, they felt free to say whatever they wanted, face-to-face and in a normal tone of voice—the same way you might talk in front of a building or a painting you find ugly. An experienced traveler, of course, "could have told by looking at my shoes that I wasn't French." And even if Sedaris were French, "it's not as if English is some mysterious tribal dialect spoken only by anthropologists and a small population of cannibals." They happen to teach it in schools all over the world. Anyone can learn it. "Even people who reportedly smell bad despite the fact that they've just taken a bath and are wearing clean clothes" ("Picka Pocketoni" 220–22).

Imagining this couple as otherwise "decent," Sedaris sounds sanguine. But as they'd used the "tiresome" word *froggy* and complained about the stench, "I was now licensed to hate [them] as much as I wanted." This, in fact, made Sedaris happy, as he'd wanted to hate them from the moment he saw them at the pole.

> Unleashed by their insults, I was now free to criticize Martin's clothing: the pleated denim shorts, the baseball cap, the T-shirt advertising a San Diego pizza restaurant. Sunglasses hung from his neck on a fluorescent cable, and the couple's bright new his-and-hers sneakers suggested that they might be headed somewhere dressy for dinner. Comfort has its place, but it seems rude to visit another country dressed as if you've come to mow its lawns.

Sounds cynical, and not at his own expense. At any rate, whereas Sedaris saw this Martin as Ugly American, Martin saw him as Stinky Frenchman. And so he'd gone from "Mr. New York City" for Bonnie to "Mr. Paris" for Bonnie's counterpart. Then again, Sedaris hadn't said a word—in either perfect English or terrible French. Nor, out of earshot, did Hugh ("Picka Pocketoni" 222).

And so Martin—nearly or at least inadvertently satirical—assumed that Sedaris was trying to rob them. "Your wallet," he warned Carol. "That joker's trying to steal your wallet. Move your pocketbook to the front where he can't get at it." Another few minutes, and he might have decided Sedaris was a crack dealer or white slaver. Still, Sedaris said nothing. If he had, Martin might apologize. And while his embarrassment would have pleased Sedaris, there'd be the awkward period that sometimes ends in a handshake. He didn't want to touch these people or see things from their perspective. "I just wanted to continue hating them" ("Picka Pocketoni" 223–24).

Martin also assumed that Sedaris couldn't be alone:

> "What you've got to understand is that these creeps are practiced professionals," he said. "I

mean, they've really got it down to an art, if you
can call that an art form."

"I wouldn't call it an art form," Carol said.
"Art is beautiful, but taking people's wallets . . .
that stinks, in my opinion."

"You've got that right," Martin said. "The
thing is that these jokers usually work in pairs."
He squinted toward the opposite end of the train.
"Odds are that he's probably got a partner
somewhere on this subway car."

"You think so?"

"I know so," he said. "They usually time it so
that one of them clips your wallet just as the train
pulls into the station. The other guy's job is to run
interference and trip you up once you catch wind of
what's going on. Then the train stops, the door
opens, and they disappear into the crowd. If Stinky
there had gotten his way, he'd probably be halfway
to Timbuktu by now. I mean, make no mistake,
these guys are fast."

"It just gets my goat," Martin added. "I mean, where's a
policioni when you need one?" *Policioni?* thought Sedaris.
Where did this asshole think he was?

I tried to imagine Martin's conversation with a
French policeman and pictured him waving his
arms, shouting, "That man tried to picka my
frienda's pocketoni!" I very much wanted to hear
such a conversation.

This sounds even more cynical, and—once again—not at
his own expense. At any rate, Hugh came up from behind
and tapped Sedaris on the shoulder, indicating that the
next stop was theirs. "There you go," said Martin. "That's
him, that's the partner. Didn't I tell you he was around

here somewhere?" ("Picka Pocketoni" 224–26, ellipsis original).

Martin, of course, was mistaken—except, perhaps, about the smell. Sedaris isn't French. Neither Sedaris nor Hugh is a thief. Nor do the two of them work as partners in crime. They do, however—notwithstanding such fights as prompted the nudist adventure, or even other problems I'll deal with in "Hugh"—work as life partners. Or as Sedaris himself puts it, as "finicky little boyfriends"—one stereotype of which (unless *I'm* mistaken) Martin, like young Marcel, was woefully unaware ("Picka Pocketoni" 227).

Spending much of his time watching movies, instead of either writing satire or studying French, Sedaris finds it odd—yet reassuring—that others there do so as well:

> I sometimes wonder why I even bothered with French class. "I am truly delighted to make your acquaintance," "I heartily thank you for this succulent meal"—I have yet to use either of these pleasantries. Since moving to Paris my most often used phrase is "One place, please." That's what one says at the box office when ordering a ticket, and I say it quite well. In New York I'd go to the movies three or four times a week. Here I've upped it to six or seven, mainly because I'm too lazy to do anything else. Fortunately, going to the movies seems to suddenly qualify as an intellectual accomplishment, on a par with reading a book or devoting time to serious thought. It's not that the movies have gotten any more strenuous, it's just that a lot of people are as lazy as I am, and together we've decided to lower the bar. ("The City of Light in the Dark" 207)

Or have they? Sedaris, here, is watching American films in English: *The Alamo, The Bridge over the River Kwai,*

Oklahoma! Brazil, Nashville. At least the natives are working on a—for them—foreign language.

Natives can, however, be just as bad as Sedaris when it comes not to laziness, and not to selfishness, but to "inhumanity." This equivalence struck Sedaris when he and Hugh attended a fair. They'd been walking down the midway—shades of Sedaris and Dan back in North Carolina—when he noticed one of the rides frozen in mid motion, "several of the passengers just dangling there." At first this didn't seem unusual, "as the creators of these rides seemed to have taken the extra step in making their attractions just that much more hideous than they needed to be." But after turning to watch a blue-faced teenager projectile vomit against the side of a taffy stand, Sedaris noticed both that the ride still wasn't moving and that a crowd—of Chinese or at least New York proportions—had gathered. He also noticed one passenger in particular:

> I don't know what happens to people when this ride is working, but when it isn't, the passengers hang in the air at odd angles, harnessed into legless metal love seats. A couple lay twelve feet off the ground, their seat back stuck in a horizontal position, staring up at the sky as if undergoing some kind of examination. Higher up, maybe fifty feet in the air, a young woman with long blond hair was hanging facedown, held in place by nothing but the harness that now strained against her weight. The couple at least had each other; it was the young woman who seemed the most likely candidate for tragedy. The crowd moved closer, and if the other three to four hundred people were anything like me, they watched the young woman and thought of the gruesome story they'd eventually relate to friends over drinks or dinner.

> In the not-too-distant future, whenever the
> conversation turned to the subject of fairs or
> amusement parks, I'd wait until my companions
> had finished their mediocre anecdotes and then, at
> just the right moment, almost as an afterthought,
> I'd say, "I once saw a girl fall to her death from one
> of those rides."

Those hundreds of people, I imagine, were *a lot* like Sedaris ("I Almost Saw This Girl Get Killed" 231, 232–33).

Police arrived, shouting that this wasn't a show. "Well of course it's not," thought Sedaris. "But that shouldn't diminish my investment." They tried moving the crowd away, "just to make room for some alleged firetruck or ambulance" ("I Almost Saw This Girl Get Killed" 234). Having been there first, the crowd stood its ground. So more police arrived, shoving everyone back onto the midway. But the view from there was blocked.

Sedaris never did learn what happened. Maybe the girl got killed. Maybe she was rescued. Maybe neither, a surreal possibility—or mental picture—that enables her, even more than Martin, to symbolize (for the reader) the kind of satirist Sedaris (as a writer) is not. Except, of course, for targets like Lois, Jon, and Martin. Anyway, the essay concludes, "it had been the young blond woman who'd wound up with the most disturbing story."

> We might have watched her, hanging by a strap
> umpteen feet in the air, but, even worse, she had
> been forced to watch us. Squinting down at our
> hideous, expectant faces, she probably saw no real
> reason to return to earth and reclaim her life
> among scumbags like us. For all I know, she might
> still be there, hovering above Paris and kicking,
> scratching at anyone who tries to get near her.
> ("I Almost Saw This Girl Get Killed" 238)

Unlike Martin, that is, she's *entitled* to cynicism at other
people's expense.

Outside of Paris, with Hugh away, one final experience enabled Sedaris to see himself as a guest far less
monstrous than Bonnie must have: not as some "moron,"
nor as "Mr. New York City," nor as a stinky, thieving Frenchman, nor a lazy good-for-nothing, nor a scumbag. This
guest, erroneously though not unreasonably, saw Sedaris
the way he'd seen those demanding, murderous drivers:
as a maniac.

Late one night, Sedaris was in what serves as their
country home's combination kitchen/living room, piecing
together a "Visible Man." They'd bought the model for the
son of a friend, some thirteen-year-old who pronounced it
null, or "worthless, unacceptable."

> The summer before, he'd wanted to be a doctor, but
> over the next few months he seemed to have
> changed his mind, deciding instead that he might
> like to design shoes.

Sounds gay. Anyway, Sedaris liked it. The body was clear
plastic, "a shell for the organs, which ranged in color from
bright red to a dull, liverish purple." Suddenly, there was
a noise. The noise, he knew, was of an injured mouse—
caught in some trap. Sedaris retrieved the mouse. Using
a bucket of water on the porch, he then started putting
it out of its misery when a van pulled up. This driver—
"Dutch, I thought, or maybe Scandinavian"—needed direc-
tions. "Oh," he said. "I see that you have a little swimming
mouse." The two went in to find a map, at which point,
for Sedaris, *self*-estrangement began ("Nuit of the Living
Dead" 249, 253, 254).

"An unexpected and unknown visitor," he writes (much
like Eichenbaum, Shklovsky, or Brecht), "allows you to see
a familiar place as if for the very first time."

I'm thinking of the meter reader rooting through the kitchen at eight A.M., the Jehovah's Witness suddenly standing in your living room. "Here," they seem to say. "Use *my* eyes. The focus is much keener."

Sedaris doesn't appear to have thought of Bonnie. Nor, for that matter, of Dinah the whore. At any rate, although he'd always thought of that room as cheerful, there was the Visible Man on the table. The pieces thereof "lay in the shadow of a large taxidermied chicken that seemed to be regarding them, determining which organ might be the most appetizing." And while the table itself was pleasant to look at—hand-hewn oak—the surrounding chairs were mismatched and in various states of disrepair:

> On the back of one hung a towel marked with the emblem of the Los Angeles County Coroner's Office. It had been a gift, not bought personally, but still it was there, leading the eye to an adjacent daybed, upon which lay two copies of a sordid true-crime magazine I purportedly buy to help me with my French. The cover of the latest issue pictured a young Belgian woman, a camper beaten to death with a cinder block. IS THERE A SERIAL KILLER IN *YOUR* REGION? the headline asked. The second copy was opened to the crossword puzzle I'd attempted earlier in the evening. One of the clues translated to "female sex organ," and in the space provided I had written the word for *vagina*.

It was the first time Sedaris had ever answered a French crossword puzzle question, and in celebration he had marked the margins with bright exclamation points ("Nuit of the Living Dead" 254, 255, emphasis original).

There seemed to be a theme developing, and everything Sedaris saw—through the Dutch Scandinavian's eyes—appeared to substantiate it: the almanac of firearms "suddenly prominent on the bookshelf," the meat cleaver "lying for no apparent reason upon a photograph of our neighbor's grandchild," the meat hooks "hanging from the clotted black interior" of the hearth. "So," the man asked, "you say you have a map?"

> I had several, and pulled the most detailed from a drawer containing, among other things, a short length of rope and a novelty pen resembling a dismembered finger. *Where does all this stuff come from?* I asked myself. There's a low cabinet beside the table, and pushing aside the delicate skull of a baby monkey, I spread the map upon the surface, identifying the road outside our house and then the village the man was looking for. It wasn't more than ten miles away. The route was fairly simple, but still I offered him the map, knowing he would feel better if he could refer to it on the road.

"Oh no," he said, "I couldn't." But Sedaris insisted ("Nuit of the Living Dead" 255, 256).

Of course, he's not a maniac—just as he isn't a thief. Just as, moreover, the guest may be neither Dutch nor Scandinavian. Still, where *does* it all come from? Most stuff, aside from the towel and meat hooks, from Paris—"bought personally" by Sedaris himself. He'd only moved there in the first place, we're told in that other essay, because of the "inevitable sense of helplessness," because of "the smoking," and because of "the shopping." And by "shopping," he meant things like: "a two-hundred-year-old wax model of a vagina, complete with human pubic hair," a "two-headed calf skull," an "ashtray in the shape of a protracted molar," "somebody's gallstone, labeled and displayed on an elegant stand," and a "suede fetus complete with umbilical cord" ("See You Again Yesterday" 155, 157, 161–62). In other words, body parts—both human and animal—or representations thereof. So by "shopping," he must also mean that finger pen, that monkey skull, and, of course, the Visible Man, which—much as the naked body symbolized people as we really are, beneath "costumes" and so beyond stereotype or satire—now symbolized, for Sedaris, people beneath the skin. It symbolized, that is, organisms that can be dismembered either surgically or satirically and, then, with any luck—or skill—reassembled. Reassembled, that is, by the reader, who knows, for example, to combine the benevolence of Sedaris on the porch (mouse drowning) with the malevolence or "inhumanity" at the fair (girl gazing) and come up with an individual. After all, Sedaris himself never does finish that model. Nor, it seems, did he even plan to. "When the sun came up," concludes this essay, "I would bury my dead and fill the empty bucket with hydrangeas, a bit of life and color, so perfect for the table. So pleasing to the eye" ("Nuit of the Living Dead" 257).

Uncle Money

Sedaris would abuse children he doesn't know, but both nurture and spoil ones he does. Like father, like mother, like son.

So far, however, such nurturing has been inept. At twenty-three, Sedaris tried parenting twelve-year-old Paul. "Fuck you," the boy had said. In other words: "Not with Lou around." Paul did, however, like being "enthused" by Sedaris—getting wound up, according to Sharon ("Rooster at the Hitchin' Post" 177). You know, brother stuff.

At twenty-six, Sedaris tried parenting nine-year-old Brandi. He'd been "roughing it" in Raleigh—slumming, according to Sharon. "You live in bad neighborhoods," she'd say, "so you can feel superior" ("The Girl Next Door" 109). In other words: "You're still a snob." Brandi's mother, however, never used shame that way. She'd simply abuse the girl, both physically and emotionally:

> The woman worked nights and left her daughter alone from four in the afternoon until two or

three in the morning. Both were blond, their hair
almost white, with invisible eyebrows and lashes.
The mother darkened hers with pencil, but the girl
appeared to have none at all. Her face was like the
weather in one of those places with no discernible
seasons. Every now and then, the circles beneath
her eyes would shade to purple. She might show up
with a fat lip or a scratch on her neck but her features betrayed nothing.

You had to feel sorry for a girl like that. No
father, no eyebrows, and that mother. Our
apartments shared a common wall, and every
night I'd hear the woman stomping home from
work. Most often she was with someone, but
whether alone or with company she'd find some
excuse to bully her daughter out of bed. Brandi had
left a doughnut on the TV or Brandi had forgotten
to drain her bathwater. They're important lessons
to learn, but there's something to be said for
leading by example.

Their apartments shared a porch as well, with one door
leading to Brandi's bedroom and another leading to his. At
any rate: no father, no real mother, and—including one in
its original wrapping—no real toys:

The only thing she owned, the only thing special,
was a foot-tall doll in a clear plastic carrying case.
It was a dime-store version of one of those Dolls
from Many Countries, this one Spanish with a beet
red dress and a droopy mantilla on her head.
Behind her, printed on cardboard, was the place
where she lived: a piñata-lined street snaking up
the hill to a dusty bullring.

The doll had been given to Brandi by her maternal grandmother, forty years old and living in a trailer beside an

army base. In the picture the girl showed Sedaris, the woman—nicknamed Rascal—was in cutoffs and an anklet:

> "We don't talk to her anymore," Brandi had said when I handed back the picture. "She's out of our life, and we're glad of it." Her voice was dull and robotic, and I got the impression that the line had been fed to her by her mother. She used a similar tone when introducing her doll. "She's not for playing with. She's for display."

No father, no mother, and, now, no grandmother (107–8, 110–11).

No wonder Brandi glommed onto Sedaris, a seemingly good pseudo-parent who included her within a tight routine:

> I had a part-time construction job and would return home at exactly 5:30. Five minutes later Brandi would knock on my door, and stand there blinking until I let her in.

Once in, she'd talk. He'd teach—or try to:

> "See," Brandi said one day, "she's on her way home to cook up those clams."
> She was talking about the castanets dangling from the doll's wrist. It was a funny thought, childish, and I probably should have let it go rather than playing the know-it-all. "If she were an American doll those might be clams," I said. "But instead she's from Spain, and those are called castanets." I wrote the word on a piece of paper. "Castanets, look it up."
> "She's not from Spain, she's from Fort Bragg."

He'd also have her draw:

I was going through a little wood-carving phase at the time, whittling figures whose heads resembled the various tools I had worked with during the day: a hammer, a hatchet, a wire brush. Before beginning, I'd arrange some paper and colored pencils on my desk. "Draw your doll," I'd say. "Copy the bullring in her little environment. Express yourself!" I encouraged Brandi to broaden her horizons, but she usually quit after the first few minutes, claiming it was too much work.

At 6:55 he'd have her leave, unless the carving went slowly and there weren't many shavings to sweep. In that case, Brandi could stay another minute:

> "Why do I have to go right this second?" she asked one evening. "Are you going to work or something?"
> "Well, no, not exactly."
> "Then what's your hurry?"

He never should have told her. The good part about being obsessive is that you're always on time for work. The bad part, you're on time for everything. "Rinsing your coffee cup, taking a bath, walking your clothes to the Laundromat: there's no mystery to your comings and goings, no room for spontaneity." At that point in his life, Sedaris went to an International House of Pancakes every evening, heading over on his bicycle at exactly seven and returning home at exactly nine. He never ate there, just drank coffee, "facing the exact same direction in the exact same booth and reading library books for exactly an hour." After this, he would ride to the grocery store—"even if I didn't need anything I'd go, because that's what that time was allotted for." If the lines were short, he'd bike home the long way or circle the block a few times, unable to return early, "as those five or ten minutes weren't scheduled for apartment time" ("The Girl Next Door" 111–13, 114).

This routine was fine by the mother, who'd found a free babysitter. It was also fine by Sedaris—in part because, even before her death, he could impersonate Sharon, in part because he *was* a snob. Poverty having lent his own "dabblings" a much-needed veneer of authenticity, he could now repay the debt "by gently lifting the lives of those around me, not en masse but one by one, the old-fashioned way." It was, he thought, "the least I could do." The routine was fine by him, that is, until Brandi—with Sedaris at either the restaurant or the store—started stealing: little things like pencil erasers, a key ring, a box of tacks. Even he knew this was a cry for nurture, a demand for both punishment and absolution, but he botched the job of meeting that demand—the job of shaming. Like Sharon, he should have "snapped" but then—in due time—made Brandi feel not pitied but loved again. ("You had to feel sorry for a girl like that.") He should, moreover, have kept it private. Instead, he threatened to snitch:

> When I confronted Brandi, she broke down immediately. It was as if she'd been dying to confess, had rehearsed it, even. The stammered apology, the plea for mercy. She hugged me around the waist, and when she finally pulled away I felt my shirtfront, expecting to find it wet with tears. It wasn't. I don't know why I did what I did next, or rather, I guess I do. It was all part of my ridiculous plan to set a good example. "You know what we have to do now, don't you?" I sounded firm and fair until I considered the consequences, at which point I faltered. "We've got to go . . . and tell your mother what you just *did?*"

Sedaris hoped Brandi might talk him out it. But she just shrugged. So he did snitch. He went and told the mother—in public. (Some man was there with her, cleaning his fingernails and watching television.) This made the woman angry—at Sedaris, though, not at Brandi:

> "So she took a pencil eraser," Brandi's mother said. "What do you want me to do, dial nine-one-one?" She made it sound unbelievable petty.
> "I just thought you should know what happened," I said.
> "Well, lucky me. Now I know."
> I returned to my apartment and pressed my ear against the bedroom wall. "Who was that?" the guy asked.
> "Oh, just some asshole."

"What did you expect that mother to do," Sharon would ask, "needlepoint a sampler with the Ten Commandments? Wake up, Dopey, the woman's a whore" ("The Girl Next Door" 109, 115, 116, emphasis and ellipsis original).

Sedaris then withheld either love or pity far too long and for the wrong reason. He was angry at the mother, not at Brandi:

> Things cooled down after that. I could forgive Brandi for breaking into my apartment, but I could not forgive her mother. *Just some asshole.* I wanted to go to the place where she worked and burn it down. In relating the story, I found myself employing lines I'd probably heard on public radio. "Children *want* boundaries," I said. "They *need* them." It sounded sketchy to me, but everyone seemed to agree—especially my mother, who suggested that in this particular case, a five-by-eleven cell might work. She wasn't yet placing the

entire blame on me, so it was enjoyable to tell her
things, to warm myself in the comforting glow of
her outrage.

> The next time Brandi knocked I pretended to
be out—a ploy that fooled no one. She called my
name, figured out where this was headed, and then
went home to watch TV. I didn't plan to stay mad
forever. A few weeks of the silent treatment and
then I figured we'd pick up where we left off.

He figured wrong. Sedaris would pass Brandi in the front
yard and ask, "How's it going?" She'd give him a tight little
smile, "the sort you'd offer if someone you hated was walking around with chocolate stains on the back of his pants."
The stains, figuratively speaking, were slides of his artwork—pages of them—that Brandi had stolen and then,
using a pin, defaced:

> "Yur a ashole," one of them read. "Suk my dick
why don't you." The spelling was all over the place,
the writing tiny and furious, bleeding into the
mind-bending designs spewed by mental patients
who don't know when to stop.

It was the exact effect Sedaris had been striving for in
his "imitation folk art"—those carvings—so not only did
he feel violated, he felt "jealous." Envious, rather. "I mean,
this girl"—like Gretchen or, later, Tiffany—"was the real
thing" ("The Girl Next Door" 117, 118, emphasis original).

> Beyond the vandalism, who knew what Brandi
planned:

> I thought things couldn't get much worse, and
then, that evening, they did. I was just returning
from the IHOP and was on the landing outside
Brandi's door when I heard her whisper, "Faggot."
She had her mouth to the keyhole, and her voice

was puny and melodic. It was the way I'd always imagined a moth might sound. "Faggot. What's the matter, faggot? What's wrong, huh?"

She laughed as I scrambled into my apartment, and then she ran to the porch and began to broadcast through my bedroom door. "Little faggot, little tattletale. You think you're so smart, but you don't know shit."

Sharon knew:

"That's it," my mother said. "We've got to get you out of there." There was no talk of going to the police or social services, just "Pack up your things. She won."

"But can't I . . ."

"Oh-ho no," my mother said. "You've got her mad now and there's no turning back. All she has to do is go to the authorities, saying you molested her. Is that what you want? One little phone call and your life is ruined."

"But I didn't do *anything*. I'm gay, remember?"

"That's not going to save you," she said. "Push comes to shove and who do you think they're going to believe, a nine-year-old girl or the full-grown man who gets his jollies carving little creatures out of balsa wood?"

"They're *not* little creatures!" I yelled. "They're tool people!"

"What the hell difference does it make? In the eyes of the law you're just some nut with a knife who sits in the pancake house staring at a goddam stopwatch. You dress that girl in something other than a tube top and prop her up on the witness stand—crying her eyes out—and what do you think is going to happen? Get that mother in on the act

and you've got both a criminal trial *and* a civil suit
on your hands."

"You watch too much TV."

"Not as much as they do," she said. "I can
guaran-goddam-tee you that. You think these
people can't smell money?"

"But I haven't got any."

"It's not your money they'll be after," she said.
"It's mine."

"You mean Dad's." I was smarting over the
"little creatures" comment and wanted to hurt her,
but it didn't work.

"I mean *our* money," she said. "You think I
don't know how these things work? I wasn't just
born some middle-aged woman with a nice purse
and a decent pair of shoes. My God, the things you
don't know. My *God*." ("The Girl Next Door" 120–21,
emphasis and ellipsis original)

The story—as told by Sedaris—begins shortly thereafter.
The essay, rather:

"Well, that little experiment is over," my
mother said. "You tried it, it didn't work out, so
what do you say we just move on." She was dressed
in her roll-up-the-shirtsleeves outfit: the faded
turquoise skirt, a cotton head scarf, and one of the
sporty blouses my father had bought in the hope
she might take up golf. "We'll start with the
kitchen," she said. "That's always the best way,
isn't it."

I was moving again. This time because of the
neighbors.

"Oh, no," my mother said. "They're not to
blame. Let's be honest now." She liked to take my
problems back to the source, which was usually me.

Like, for instance, when I got food poisoning it wasn't the chef's fault. *"You're* the one who wanted to go Oriental. *You're* the one who ordered the lomain."

"Lo mein. It's two words."

"Oh, he speaks Chinese now! Tell me, Charlie Chan, what's the word for six straight hours of vomiting and diarrhea?"

What she meant was that I'd tried to save money. The cheap Chinese restaurant, the seventy-five-dollar-a-month apartment: "Cut corners and it'll always come back to bite you in the ass." That was one of her sayings. But if you didn't *have* money how could you *not* cut corners?

"And whose fault is it that you don't have any money? I'm not the one who turned up his nose at a full-time job. I'm not the one who spends his entire paycheck down at the hobby shop."

"I understand that."

"Well, good," she said, and then we began to wrap the breakables. (105–6, emphasis original)

Notice Sharon's refusal to shame, having done enough of that already. Notice, too, her instruction: "What do you say we just move on?"

The essay ends there as well—not, however, with Sharon and Sedaris but with Sharon and Brandi:

My new apartment was eight blocks away, facing our city's first Episcopal church. My mother paid the deposit and the first month's rent and came with her station wagon to help me pack and move my things. Carrying a box of my feather-weight balsa-wood sculptures out onto the landing, her hair gathered beneath a gingham scarf, I wondered how she appeared to Brandi, who was

certainly watching through the keyhole. What
did she represent to her? The word *mother* wouldn't
do, as I don't really think she understood what it
meant. A person who shepherds you along the way
and helps you out when you're in trouble—what
would she call that thing? A queen? A crutch? A
teacher?

I heard a noise from behind the door, and then
the little moth voice. "Bitch," Brandi whispered.

I fled back into the apartment, but my mother
didn't even pause. "Sister," she said, "you don't
know the half of it." ("The Girl Next Door" 121–22)

Notice, once again, Sharon's refusal to shame, which—with
no connection to Brandi, no love reciprocated—couldn't
have done the trick. Notice too, once again, her instruction—"Sister, you don't know the half of it"—which could
have.

At any rate, what *would* you call such a thing? Not
bitch, but—once again—virago. To cite—but reject—a sex-
ist definition: "a bold, impudent (or wicked) woman; a ter-
magant, a scold." Look it up. To cite a feminist: "Virago has
come to mean bitch because people prefer to forget what
it really means: a woman of great stature, strength, and
courage who is not feminine in the conventional ways"
(King 218).

In New York, the only child we hear about is neither
abused, nurtured, nor spoiled by Sedaris. He's just a brat.
A brat, moreover, who humiliated a caretaker and so reminds Sedaris of himself. ("I don't need your filthy chickens," he'd told Lena. "We buy our own—from the store"
["The Curly Kind" 163].) There's a snack food connection
as well:

I was carrying out the Rosenblatts' garbage
this afternoon when the maid from the next

apartment closed the door behind her, straightened her white uniform, and pushed the button for the elevator. This is the twelfth floor, four apartments per level and only one elevator, so it usually takes a while. I watched as the maid was joined by two young children accompanied by an Irish nanny. As they waited, the nanny reached into her canvas bag and handed the boy a bag of Cheetos, which he opened and immediately emptied onto the floor, screaming, "I wanted the CURLY kind. Don't you know ANYTHING?"

The nanny lowered her head. Sedaris and the maid locked eyes and shrugged their shoulders as if to say, "What can you do?" The elevator arrived. And they boarded, leaving behind a mat of uncurly Cheetos to be crushed by other tenants until some janitor swept them up (161–62, emphasis original).

Lena, you recall, would ask Sedaris: "Didn't you have potato chips *yesterday?*" ("Blood Work" 132, emphasis original). Sedaris in turn, in writing about that boy, is doing the job the nanny—or maid—might have: shaming him, though belatedly, for having humiliated her. This assumes, of course, both that the essay is addressed to the boy, in part, and that he's read it. In light of Sharon's pedagogical response to Brandi ("Sister, you don't know the half of it"), the essay also suggests that although Sedaris was too disconnected—at the time—to shame the boy, he was, in fact, well positioned to instruct. Instead of shrugging "What can you do?" he should have taught some manners and not, this time, by example. The last thing anyone else should have done, that is, was clean up his mess. Once again, the essay itself—as addressed to and read by the boy—constitutes such a lesson. Other readers also shamed or instructed include ones reminded of themselves by either the boy, with those Cheetos, or Sedaris, with those chickens and chips.

In Paris, we hear about a number of children. Some—children he knows—Sedaris spoils. He does so, however, without nurturing them. In other words, he's no Aunt Monie—with the bearskin rug, not Pinocchio. Both Sedaris and Hugh, for example, spoiled that thirteen-year-old: the brat who, having decided to become a shoe designer instead of a doctor, declared their Visible Man gift *null* (worthless, unacceptable). "I suggested that he at least keep the feet," Sedaris admits, "but when he turned up his nose we gave him twenty euros and decided to keep the model ourselves" ("Nuit of the Living Dead" 249). Instead of the money, or the feet, they should have offered a lesson on rudeness. And if they'd any connection to the boy, any love or simply friendship reciprocated, they should have shamed him—without, of course, pulling a Brandi ("Listen, you little faggot . . .").

Sedaris alone—in "one of those hotels without room service"—spoiled another brat. This one, like the Rosenblatts' neighbor, was a messy American:

> Past the restaurant and gift shop, in the center of the lobby, was a complimentary beverage stand. I thought I'd get a coffee and take it outdoors, but just as I approached, a boy swooped in and began mixing himself a cup of hot chocolate. He looked like all the other kids I'd been seeing lately, in airports, in parking lots: the oversize sweatshirts stamped with team emblems, the baggy jeans and jazzy sneakers. His watch was fat and plastic, like a yo-yo strapped to his wrist, and his hair looked as if it had been cut with the lid of a can, the irregular hanks stiffened with gel and coaxed to stand at peculiar angles.

It was a complicated business, mixing a cup of hot chocolate. "You had to spread the powdered cocoa from one end of the table to the other and use as many stirrers as possible, making sure to thoroughly chew the wetted ends before tossing them upon the stack of unused napkins." This, though, is what Sedaris likes about children: "complete attention to one detail and complete disregard of another." When finally finished, the boy scooted over to the coffee urn, filling two cups, black, and then fitting them with lids. The drinks were stacked into a tower, then tentatively lifted off the table. "Whoa," he whispered. Hot chocolate seeped from beneath the lid of the bottom cup and ran down his hand. "Do you need some help with those?" Sedaris asked. "Yeah," he said. "Carry these upstairs." No *please*. No *thank you*. Just "I'll take the hot chocolate myself" ("Chicken in the Henhouse" 211, 215).

Sedaris, of course, did as he was told. No lesson on rudeness. And given the lack of connection, no attempt to shame. In the end, it was the boy's mother—not father—who sort of did the right thing. "You people run a very nice hotel," she told Sedaris—and then gave him a dollar ("Chicken in the Henhouse" 224). Not bad, though Martin the diabetic—in that other case of mistaken identity—had been far more generous.

Sedaris spoils Madelyn as well, beginning the day she was born. People who have nothing to prove, he writes, offer practical baby gifts: "sturdy cotton rompers made to withstand the cycle of vomit and regular washing." People competing for the title Best-Loved Uncle, however, "send satin pants and delicate hand-crafted sweaters accompanied by notes reading 'P.S. The fur collar is detachable'" ("Baby Einstein" 242). *Best-Loved Uncle*. In other words: "Uncle Money," a both ridiculous and self-critical title Sedaris does, in fact, give himself. (His own money now, not Sharon's.) Once again, though, he's no Aunt Monie. Or rather, he's someone who'd give the girl Pinocchio but not ask—either in public or in private—if lying is something *she* likes to do. But at least he's also someone whose avuncular behavior, in reality, is completely unlike alter ego Chug's: twisting the meat of nephew Marty's thigh, popping him across the face. You know, physical abuse.

Sedaris can, however, physically abuse girls he doesn't know. Or at least can *imagine* them killed—if envious. Such abuse—such inhumanity, rather—is therefore motivated by selfishness. Take, for example, the sisters to whom both he and Hugh would one day lose their home. As with the blond at the fair or, more to the point, his own sister Gretchen ("I didn't want to kill her, but hoped someone else might do the job" ["Twelve Moments in the Life of the Artist" 42]), Sedaris fantasizes their demise. The essay begins:

> "Finding an apartment is a lot like falling in love," the real estate agent told us. She was a stylish grandmother in severe designer sunglasses. Dyed blond hair, black stockings, a little scarf tied just so around the throat: for three months she drove us around Paris in her sports car, Hugh up front and me folded like a lawn chair into the backseat.
>
> At the end of every ride I'd have to teach myself to walk all over again, but that was just a minor physical complaint. My problem was that I already loved an apartment. The one we had was perfect, and searching for another left me feeling faithless and sneaky, as if I were committing adultery. After a viewing, I'd stand in our living room, looking up at the high, beamed ceiling and trying to explain that the other two-bedroom had meant nothing to me. Hugh took the opposite tack

and blamed the apartment for making us cheat. We'd offered, practically begged, to buy it, but the landlord was saving the place for his daughters, two little girls who would eventually grow to evict us. Our lease could be renewed for another fifteen years, but Hugh refused to waste his love on a lost cause. When told our apartment could never truly be ours, he hung up the phone and contacted the real estate grandmother, which is what happens when you cross him: he takes action and moves on.

The place was dead to him, Sedaris adds, "but I kept hoping for a miracle." A riding accident, a playhouse fire—"lots of things can happen to little girls" ("Possession" 180–81).

Or take Anne Frank. But before we do, let's take Sedaris on other—living—Dutch children. Santa Claus is supposed to give American brats not toys but coal, shameful punishment for bad behavior. Of course, most get toys anyway. Dutch brats, however, shouldn't expect toys. Nor, Sedaris was told, should they expect coal. They expect, instead, to be abused by both Saint Nicholas and his slaves. ("YOU ARE NOT SANTA'S SLAVE," Sedaris had been taught by Macy's ["SantaLand Diaries" 173, emphasis original].) Sorry, *ex*-slaves:

> While our Santa flies in on a sled, the Dutch version arrives [from Spain] by boat and then transfers to a white horse. The event is televised, and great crowds gather at the waterfront to greet him. I'm not sure if there's a set date, but he generally docks in late November and spends a few weeks hanging out and asking people what they want.
>
> "Is it just him alone?" I asked. "Or does he come with some backup?"

Oscar's English was close to perfect, but he seemed thrown by a term normally reserved for police reinforcement.

"Helpers," I said. "Does he have any elves?"

Sedaris couldn't help feel personally insulted when Oscar—unaware of both Macy's and elf-consciousness—denounced the very idea as silly and unrealistic. But the words *silly* and *unrealistic* were redefined when Sedaris learned that Saint Nicholas travels with "six to eight black men." The six to eight black men, moreover, had been characterized as "personal slaves" until the political climate changed in the 1950s and it was decided that instead of being slaves they were just good friends. History, however, has proved that "something usually comes *between* slavery and friendship, a period of time marked not by cookies and quiet hours beside the fire but by bloodshed and mutual hostility." And they do have such violence in the Netherlands. But rather than duking it out among themselves, Sedaris imagines, Saint Nicholas and his six to eight black men must have decided to take it out on the public. Because in the early years if a child was naughty, they would beat him with what Oscar described as "the small branch of a tree." "A switch?" asked Sedaris:

> "Yes," he said. "That's it. They'd kick him and beat him with a switch. Then if the youngster was really bad, they'd put him in a sack and take him back to Spain."
>
> "Saint Nicholas would *kick* you?"
>
> "Well, not anymore," Oscar said. "Now he just *pretends* to kick you."
>
> He considered this to be progressive, but in a way I think it's almost more perverse than the original punishment. "I'm going to hurt you but not really." How many times have we fallen for that

line? The fake slap invariably makes contact,
adding the elements of shock and betrayal to what
had previously been plain old-fashioned fear. What
kind of Santa spends his time pretending to kick
people before stuffing them into a canvas sack?
Then, of course, you've got the six to eight former
slaves who could potentially go off at any moment.

This last bit is, of course, ironic. The concern expressed,
like that slap, is fake—in part because most of these children don't believe in Saint Nicholas. In part because, for
those who do, such abuse is emotional, not physical. (No
one really gets kicked, let alone pretend kicked.) In part
because Sedaris doesn't know any. He's disconnected—no
interest or investment. And so he can afford to be amused.
But I shouldn't say *emotional* abuse. Both fear and distress, according to Tomkins, are affects ("Six to Eight Black
Men" 160–62, emphasis original).

At any rate, we all know what happened to Anne along
with her own sister. Such knowledge, however, doesn't stop
Sedaris from coveting *their* apartment when he and Hugh,
on break from the Paris search, visit Amsterdam:

On our first afternoon we took a walk and
came across the Anne Frank House, which was a
surprise. I'd had the impression she lived in a
dump, but it's actually a very beautiful seventeenth-
century building right on the canal. Tree-lined
street, close to shopping and public transportation:
in terms of location it was perfect. My months of
house hunting had caused me to look at things in
a certain way, and on seeing the crowd gathered
at the front door, I did not think, *Ticket line,* but,
Open house!
We entered the annex behind the famous
bookcase, and on crossing the threshold, I felt what

the grandmother had likened to being struck by lightning, an absolute certainty that this was the place for me. That it would be mine. The entire building would have been impractical and far too expensive, but the part where Anne Frank and her family had lived, their triplex, was exactly the right size and adorable, which is something they never tell you. In plays and movies it always appears drab and old ladyish, but open the curtains and the first words that come to mind are not, "I still believe all people are really good at heart" but "Who do I have to knock off in order to get this apartment?"

Clearly, you knocked Anne off. Clearly, too, Sedaris wasn't being good at heart—or benevolent. Hugh was, though. While Sedaris raced around imagining the renovation, deciding where to put his office, Hugh—stopping to examine the movie-star portraits glued to Anne's bedroom wall, "a wall that I personally would have knocked down"— imagined what it must have been like there for her ("Possession" 184, 185).

"I was in a fever," writes Sedaris. But then he wandered into some museum next door, saw the Primo Levi quote emblazoned there on a wall—

A SINGLE ANNE FRANK MOVES US MORE THAN THE COUNTLESS OTHERS WHO SUFFERED JUST AS SHE DID BUT WHOSE FACES HAVE REMAINED IN THE SHADOWS. PERHAPS IT IS BETTER THAT WAY. IF WE WERE CAPABLE OF TAKING IN ALL THE SUFFERING OF ALL THOSE PEOPLE, WE WOULD NOT BE ABLE TO LIVE.

—and "snapped" out of it. Or did he? The essay ends:

He did not specify that we would not be able to live *in her house,* but it was implied, and it effectively squashed any fantasy of ownership. The

added tragedy of Anne Frank is that she almost
made it, that she died along with her sister just
weeks before their camp was liberated. Having
already survived two years in hiding, she and
her family might have stayed put and lasted out
the war were it not for a neighbor, never identified,
who turned them in. I looked out the window,
wondering who could have done such a thing, and
caught my reflection staring back at me. Then,
beyond that, across the way, I saw the most
beautiful apartment. ("Possession" 185–87,
emphasis original)

So maybe he "snapped" only afterwards, perhaps as late as
the writing of "Possession." Because instead of really looking at and therefore hating himself, as Sharon both suggested and *instructed* that day after Halloween, he simply
looked away, beyond that reflection. Sedaris blinded himself—for now—to the obvious fact that *he* could have done
such a thing.

Or did he? Maybe Sedaris—both to punish himself
and to make the reader, if possible, hate him as well—is
pretending to have looked away. (Not a lie, exactly—an
indicated mask.) But it's impossible for us to do so, as he
himself must recognize. Once again, we don't really know
Sedaris—despite that encounter of ours in Des Moines
(see "David"). We don't know the man who could say of
Alisha: "Like all of my friends, she's a lousy judge of
character" ("City of Angels" 126). We only know the one
who—as a joke—writes such a thing. Or rather, the one
written by it: not Sedaris, but "Sedaris"—his best, perhaps most authentic self. Because in piecing "Sedaris"
together as both narrator and *literary* character, Sedaris,
like any author, omits not the feet but, figuratively speaking, the asshole—even, or especially, when confessing such

behavior. And so, in a way, we're like that middleman in New York: "If something was stolen, or alleged to have been stolen, it was he who defended our character" ("Blood Work" 123).

Of course, there's nothing original about positing such a distinction: Sedaris vs. "Sedaris." Authors themselves do it. (Even Sedaris does. In "After Malison"—see "[Your Name Here]." In "Me Talk Pretty One Day"—"I was determined to create some sort of identity for myself: David the hard worker, David the cut-up" [171].) Take, for example, La Rochefoucauld on autobiographical speech: "Desire to talk about ourselves and to show our failings from the viewpoint we ourselves would choose, accounts for a great deal of our candor" (383). Take J. D. Salinger—or "Buddy Glass"—on autobiographical or rather confessional *text:*

> A confessional passage has probably never been
> written that didn't stink a little bit of the writer's
> pride in having given up his pride. The thing to
> listen for, every time, with a public confessor, is
> what he's *not* confessing to. At a certain period of
> his life (usually, grievous to say, a *successful*
> period), a man may suddenly feel it Within His
> Power to confess that he cheated on his final exams
> at college, he may even choose to reveal that
> between the ages of twenty-two and twenty-four
> he was sexually impotent, but these gallant
> confessions in themselves are no guarantee that
> we'll find out whether he once got piqued at his
> pet hamster and stepped on its head. (195,
> emphasis original)

Take Proust on all text: "A book is the product of a different self"—though not, of course, an *entirely* different self—"from the one we manifest in our habits, in our social life, in our vices" (*Against Sainte-Beuve,* quoted in Painter 2: 6). Books, for example, by Bergotte—a character he based, in part, on Anatole France (1844–1924):

> A kind of austerity of taste which he had, a kind of determination to write nothing of which he could not say that it was "mellow," which had made people for so many years regard him as a sterile and precious artist, a chiseller of trifles, was on the contrary the secret of his strength, for habit forms the style of the writer just as much as the character of the man, and the author who has more than once been content to attain, in the expression of his thoughts, to a certain kind of attractiveness, in so doing lays down unalterably the boundaries of his talent, just as, in succumbing too often to pleasure, to laziness, to the fear of being put to trouble, one traces for oneself, on a character which it will finally be impossible to retouch, the lineaments of one's vices and the limits of one's virtue.

> If, however, despite all the similarities which I was to perceive later on between the writer and the man, I had not at first sight, in Mme Swann's drawing-room, believed that this could be Bergotte, the author of so many divine books, who stood before me, perhaps I was not altogether wrong, for he himself did not, in the strict sense of the word, "believe" it either. He did not believe it since he showed some alacrity in ingratiating himself with fashionable people (though he was not a snob), and with literary men and journalists who were vastly inferior to himself. Of course he had long since learned, from the suffrage of his readers, that he had genius, compared to which social position and official rank were as nothing. He had learned that

he had genius, but he did not believe it since he
continued to simulate deference towards mediocre
writers in order to succeed, shortly, in becoming
an Academician, when the Academy and the
Faubourg Saint-Germain have no more to do with
that part of the Eternal Mind which is the author
of the works of Bergotte than with the law of
causality or the idea of God. That also he knew,
but as a kleptomaniac knows, without profiting by
the knowledge, that it is wrong to steal. And the
man with the goatee beard and snail-shell nose
knew and used all the tricks of the gentleman
who pockets your spoons, in his efforts to reach
the coveted academic chair, or some duchess or
other who could command several votes at the
election, but to do so in a way that ensured that no
one who would consider the pursuit of such a goal
a vice in him would see what he was doing. He
was only half-successful; one could hear, alternating
with the speech of the true Bergotte, that of the
other, selfish and ambitious Bergotte who talked
only of his powerful, rich or noble friends in order
to enhance himself, he who in his books, when he
was really himself, had so well portrayed the
charm, pure as a mountain spring, of the poor.
(2: 178–80)

Take Roland Barthes on Proust:

The Proustian oeuvre brings on stage (or into
writing) an "I" [who] is not the one who remembers,
confides, confesses, he is the one who discourses.
[And so] it is vain to wonder if the book's Narrator
is Proust (in the civil meaning of the patronymic):
it is simply *another* Proust, often unknown to
himself. (*"Longtemps"* 282, emphasis original)

Better yet, take Nietzsche:

> The ceaseless desire to create on the part of the
> artist, together with his ceaseless observation of
> the world outside him, prevent him from becoming
> better and more beautiful as a person, that is to
> say from creating *himself*—except, that is, if his
> self-respect is sufficiently great to compel him to
> exhibit himself before others as being as great
> and beautiful as his works increasingly are. In
> any event, he possesses only a fixed quantity of
> strength: that of it which he expends upon
> *himself*—how could he at the same time expend it
> on his *work?*—and the reverse. (*Human, All Too
> Human* 236–37, emphasis original)

Then again, Nietzsche—like Sedaris—wasn't a parent. Nor—in class—can he have been much of a teacher.
"Can a philosopher really undertake with a good con-
science to have something to teach every day?" he asks.

> And to teach it to anyone who cares to listen?
> Will he not be obliged to give the impression of
> knowing more than he does know? Will he not be
> obliged to speak before an audience of strangers
> of things which he can safely speak of only
> amongst his nearest friends? And speaking
> generally: is he not robbing himself of his freedom
> to follow his genius whenever and wherever it calls
> him?—through being obligated to think in public
> about predetermined subjects at predetermined
> hours? And to do so before youths! (*Untimely
> Meditations* 186)

Hugh

Apart from Snowball, Sedaris likes straight and therefore supposedly real men who don't, in turn, like him. ("As has been the case for my entire life, the more someone dislikes me the more attractive he becomes" ["Full House" 37].) Needless to say, none of his boyfriends has embodied such an ideal. They present other problems as well.

The ideal—not atypical of gays—is clearly ridiculous. (See Bersani 208.) At about fourteen, when Sedaris started dreaming of classmates Walt, Dale, Brad, Scott, and Thad, not to mention well-hung Dan and broad-shouldered Chip, his alter ego, also fourteen, was writing that pornography about guys at the auto plant—not to mention "randy park rangers" ("My Manuscript" 23). In reality, Sedaris diddled a "faggot."

> There was one boy at camp I felt I might get along with, a Detroit native named Jason who slept on the bunk beneath mine. Jason tended to look

away when talking to the other boys, shifting his eyes as though he were studying the weather conditions. Like me, he used his free time to curl into a fetal position, staring at the bedside calendar upon which he'd x-ed out all the days he had endured so far. We were finishing our 7:15 to 7:45 wash-and-rinse segment one morning when our dormitory counselor arrived for inspection shouting, "What are you a bunch of goddamned faggots who can't make your beds?"

I giggled out loud at his stupidity. If anyone knew how to make a bed, it was a faggot. It was the others he needed to worry about. I saw Jason laughing, too, and soon we took to mocking this counselor, referring to each other first as "faggots" and then as "stinking faggots." We were "lazy faggots" and "sunburned faggots." We couldn't protest the word, as that would have meant acknowledging the truth of it. The most we could do was embrace it as a joke. Embodying the term in all its clichéd glory, we minced and pranced about the room for each other's entertainment when the others weren't looking. I found myself outperforming my teachers, who had failed to capture the proper spirit of loopy bravado inherent in the role. *Faggot,* as a word, was always delivered in a harsh, unforgiving tone befitting those weak or stupid enough to act upon their impulses. We used it as a joke, an accusation, and finally as a dare. Late at night I'd feel my bunk buck and sway, knowing that Jason was either masturbating or beating eggs for an omelette. *Is it me he's thinking about?* I'd follow his lead and wake the next morning to find our entire iron-frame unit had wandered a good eighteen inches away from the

wall. Our love had the power to move bunks.
("I Like Guys" 90)

So did the alter ego:

> While the imagination certainly has its
> place, I feel that it is important for a writer to back
> certain chapters with a little experience, so a few
> months ago I started hanging out in the rest room
> of JCPenney in hopes of getting just that—a little
> experience.
>
> I stood at the urinal for almost two hours
> before someone finally took the bait and gave me a
> signal that he was there to play hardball. Meeting
> his eyes I understood that I could use him as my
> research stud, fodder for my manuscript—a little
> footnote who would drive my future biographers
> wild and leave my readers breathless and hungry
> for more. Research Stud and I skipped over all the
> bullshit that everyone else goes through: the formal
> introductions, the phone calls, the dates—we just
> got to the exclamation point right there in the stall!
> Afterwards, he sort of ruined everything by telling
> me that he is a political science major at N.C. state
> and his name is Julian. I hate that name. In my
> manuscript he is named Dirk. I've made him about
> three inches taller and have given him a good, thick
> ten and one-half inches between his legs. Julian
> and I met in the rest room a few more times before
> we were interrupted by a store detective who, I am
> convinced, was interested in arranging a three-way.
> After that, we started doing it in Julian's car. He'd
> drive us out into the country and park behind an
> abandoned house set on a dirt road.
>
> Julian was all right, but nothing at all like the
> hard-driving top man I've made him out to be in my

manuscript. He was actually very stiff and uptight. We'd be doing it and I would whisper, "Talk to me, talk to me," and he'd start telling me about his summer job as a page at the state legislature building. That was not the kind of talk I was after. I asked him if he had any friends he could invite along the next time. I wanted a good mental picture of what it might be like with three or four studs at one time, ramming away and taking it all. When Julian backed off, I went to the bathroom at the Trailways station and found some real men who could help me. ("My Manuscript" 29–30)

Sedaris, I take it, is a bottom—not to mention a size queen. In fact, he also finds ridiculous the very idea of topping someone—if, that is, his sex partner embodies the ideal. The central joke of "Parade," for example, is that the narrator—another alter ego, not to mention another snob—fantasizes having screwed Norman Mailer, Charlton Heston, Peter Jennings, Bruce Springsteen, and Mike Tyson. Here's the bit on Springsteen:

I was the boss when Bruce and I were together. Maybe I should give this Patty person a call and tell her how Bruce needs to have it, give her a few pointers and clear up this "Boss" business once and for all. Tell her how Bruce groveled and begged for a commitment and how he behaved when I turned him down. I'd said, "What's the use of being a multimillionaire when you walk around dressed like a second-shift welder at U.S. Pipe & Boiler?" Bruce wants to keep in touch with his "people," which is admirable in theory but grotesque when you consider the fact that his "people" consume gasoline, domestic beer, and acne medication in equal amounts.

Bruce took it hard and picked up these women on the rebound. I remember running into that last wife of his, the model, at a party. It was she, I, Morley Safer, and Waylon Jennings. We were waiting for the elevator, and she was saying to Waylon that Bruce had just donated seven figures to charity, and I said, "No matter how much money Bruce gives to charity, I still say he's one of the tightest men I've ever known." It went right over her head, but Morley knew what I was talking about and we shared a smile.

Here's the bit on Tyson:

Mike Tyson and I were arguing over what to name the kitten we'd bought. I would have just as soon taken one of the many free kittens that had been offered to us. Everyone wanted to give Mike and me kittens. I thought we might just take one of those, but Mike said no. He wanted the kitten that had captured his heart from a pet shop window the previous week, a white Persian/Himalayan female. I don't care for puffy cats in the first place, and this one, with her flat face, reminded me of whatshername, Bruce's new girlfriend, Patty. But I said, "All right, Mike." I said, "If you want this Persian/Himalayan mix, then that's what we'll get." I can love just about anything on all fours, so I said, "Fine, whatever." ("Parade" 5–6, 8)

Like love and pity, however, desire and identification can be hard to tell apart. Sedaris may want someone like Tyson, but he also wants to *be* someone like Tyson. So fantasies of screwing like or even as Tyson—also typical of gays—aren't, for Sedaris, completely ridiculous.

"I've never gone to bed early," begins one essay, "and

have no intention of changing my schedule." (This is an
allusion to as well as a critique of Proust. *Remembrance
of Things Past* begins: "For a long time I would go to bed
early" [1: 1].) Instead, Sedaris stays up late either drowning mice or "replaying one of my current, ongoing fantasies." The fantasies are called "Mr. Science," "I've Got
a Secret," and "The Knockout." In "Mr. Science," Sedaris
cures AIDS, emphysema, and—without making a fuss
about it—cancer. ("People can once again enjoy a cigarette
after a rigorous bout of anal sex.") He also invents a reju-
venating soap that doesn't work on editors of fashion magazines, on anyone who's had too much plastic surgery, or
on television executives "whose job it is to move a program
from Sunday at eight to Wednesday at nine-thirty, then
back to Sunday and on to Thursday, all so they can sell a
few more soft-drink or taco commercials." In "I've Got a
Secret," he's "the most audacious and beautiful woman in
the world"—who also happens to write *Lolita* and then
spend the rest of her life "sleeping with professional foot-
ball players." Nabokov, he imagines, never existed ("The
Late Show" 249, 250, 252, 262, 263).

"The Knockout," however, begins:

> I'm one fight away from being named
> heavyweight boxing champion of the world, and
> still people are asking, "Who *is* this guy?" If forced
> to describe me to a police sketch artist, you might
> begin by mentioning my nose. It isn't exactly
> upturned, it isn't "pugged"; but when they're viewed
> eye to eye, you'll notice that my nostrils are
> prominent and oddly expressive, like a second,
> smaller pair of eyes assigned to keep watch over
> the lower half of my face, home to my full lips and
> perfect, luminous teeth.

He's Tyson, in other words, only white—and much better

looking. Think: Dolph Lundgren as Ivan Drago. Or Sylvester
Stallone as Rocky. Or John Loprieno in that favorite soap:

> When the sketch artist draws my eyes, you'll
> step back, saying, "No, I'm afraid that's not right at
> all." After four of five more unsuccessful attempts,
> the artist will lose his patience and remind you
> that "soulful" is not a precisely physical description.
> The difficulty comes in trying to separate my eyes
> from my eyebrows, which alter my face much the
> way that varying punctuation marks can change
> the meaning of a sentence. I've got the exclamation
> point I wear when ambushed by photographers,
> the question mark, the period I wear when I mean
> business, the dash, the thoughtful semi-colon, and
> the series of three dots I rely upon when rudely
> interrupted or when searching for just the right
> word. The eyebrows work in consort *[sic]* with
> my inky black hair, which weighs in midway
> between curly and wavy, and calls for the invention
> of a new word.
>   "It's . . . cravy," you'll say. "Like a storm at sea
> if the ocean were made out of hair instead of water."
>   When the sketch artist throws down his
> pencil, you'll say, "Okay, then, how's this: he looks
> kind of like the guy who used to play Cord Roberts
> on *One Life to Live.* Or, no, I take that back. He
> looks *exactly* like the guy who used to play Cord
> Roberts on *One Life to Live.* Is *that* descriptive
> enough for you?"

He's smarter, too:

> It's somewhat surprising that I'm a serious
> contender for the title of world heavyweight
> champion, not because I'm slow or weak but

because I'm a relative newcomer to the sport. I'd been just another Yale medical student and had never really thought of fighting until I got shut out of an endotracheal intubation seminar and signed up for a boxing class instead. The teacher recognized my extraordinary talent, lined up a few regional matches, and one thing led to another. I looked good in a hooded sweatshirt, and so when asked to go professional, I said, "Okay. Why not?"

And gay, of course:

The championship bout is five days away when the publicist discovers I have a boyfriend, who maybe doesn't look like Hugh but definitely cooks like him. I haven't been hiding my homosexuality. I've never lied or purposely avoided the question, it's just that no one has ever specifically asked. I'd never seen it as any big deal, but the news seems to change everything. Those who loved me because I was white now feel betrayed. They'd assigned me to be their representative. I was supposed to kick some black ass in their name, but now they're not sure whose side they're on.

"Which is more important," Sedaris demands, "my race or my sexual preference?" ("The Late Show" 255–56, 257, emphasis and ellipsis original).

All three fantasies, moreover, are satirical. Sedaris fans—one target—must confront their own weakness: in "The Knockout," racism, homophobia, or both. As for the other target, Sedaris himself:

In reviewing these titles, I can't help but notice a few common themes. Looks seem rather important, as does the ability to enlighten, disappoint, and control great numbers of people

who always seem to be American. In a city where
every woman over the age of fifty has blond hair,
my Mr. Science miracle soap would surely have the
Parisians lined up all the way to Bethlehem. But
it doesn't interest me to manipulate the French.
I'm not keyed in to their value system. Because
they are not my people, their imagined praise or
condemnation means nothing to me. Paris, it seems,
is where I've come to dream about America.

My epic fantasies offer the illusion of
generosity but never the real thing. I give to some
only so I can withhold from others. It's fine to cure
the leukemia sufferers but much more satisfying to
imagine the parade of opportunists confounded by
my refusal to cooperate. In imagining myself as
modest, mysterious, and fiercely intelligent, I'm
forced to realize that, in real life, I have none of
these qualities.

"Nobody," Sedaris explains, "dreams of things he already
has" ("The Late Show" 263–64).

Once again, though, desire and identification are
hard to distinguish. Sedaris may want to be someone like
Tyson—or Jennings, rather—but he also *wants* someone
like him. And so the dream date is just as attractive and
intelligent as Sedaris, in fantasy. Maybe more so. In reality, though, he'd better not be. In particular, he'd better
not be smart. Sedaris is far too insecure about as well as
too invested in "genius," literary genius in particular
(hence that *Lolita* fantasy), to withstand any such compe-
tition. Hence—recall that French *VAGINA!!!*—his passion
for crossword puzzles:

I've been told that crossword puzzles help
fight the advance of Alzheimer's Disease, but that
had nothing to do with my initiation. I started

working them a few years ago, after dropping by to visit a former boyfriend. The man was and still is exceedingly—almost painfully—handsome. In Eugene Maleska's crossword terminology, he's braw and pulchritudinous, while Will Shortz, current puzzle editor for *The New York Times,* might define him as a "wower," the clue being "Turns heads, in a way."

Because my former boyfriend was so good-looking, I had always insisted that he must also be stupid, the reason being that it was simply unfair for someone to be blessed with both chiseled features and basic conversational skills. He was, of course, much smarter than I gave him credit for, and he eventually proved his intelligence by breaking up with me. We both wound up moving to New York, where over time we developed what currently passes for a casual friendship. I stopped by his office one afternoon, hoping that maybe he'd lost a few teeth, and there he was, leaning back in his chair and finishing the Friday *New York Times* puzzle with a ballpoint pen. The capital city of Tuvalu, a long-forgotten Olympic weight lifter, a fifteen-letter word for *dervish:* "Oh, that," he said. "It's just something I do with my hands while I'm on the phone."

Sedaris was "devastated" ("21 Down" 201–2). The Friday puzzle, by the way, is the week's second hardest. Saturday's is harder.

The dream date, moreover, is sentimental—romantic even. (For more on the topic of sentimentality, please see "Eve," this volume.) Or he was back when Sharon was alive and Sedaris hadn't yet introjected her aversion to sentiment. Back, that is, when Sedaris hitchhiked:

> When I thought of sex, I pictured someone standing
> before me crying, "I love you so much that . . . I
> don't even know who I am anymore." My imaginary
> boyfriend was of no particular age or race, all that
> mattered was that he was crazy about me. Our
> first encounter would take place under bizarre
> circumstances: at the christening of a warship, or
> maybe a hurricane might bring us together in a
> crowded storm shelter. I thought about our
> courtship and the subsequent anniversaries, when
> our adopted children would gather at our feet
> saying, "Tell us again about your first date." I
> suppose we could have met in a car or van but not
> while I was hitchhiking; it would have to be more
> complicated than that. Maybe the driver of my
> vehicle would suffer a heart attack, and he would
> be one of the medics.

The important thing was that Sedaris wouldn't be looking
for it, he explains, "that's what would make it so romantic" ("Planet of the Apes" 140, ellipsis original).

By the time Sedaris met Hugh, baking pies, he'd
other—no, not ideals. Other standards. Like Sedaris back
then, Hugh was single—"which came as no great surprise,
considering that he spent his leisure time rolling out
dough and crying to George Jones albums." One problem
with Sedaris, though, "was that, according to several reli-
able sources, I tended to exhaust people" ("See You Again
Yesterday" 154). So did the alter ego who screwed both
Springsteen and Tyson:

> I would scare away my dates on the first night by
> telling them that this was *it,* the love experience
> I'd been waiting for. I would plan our futures.
> Everything we did together held meaning for me
> and would remain bright in my memory. By the

second date, I would arrive at the boyfriend's apartment carrying a suitcase and a few small pieces of furniture so that when I moved in completely I wouldn't have to hire a crew of movers. When these boyfriends became frightened and backed away, I would hire detectives to follow them. I needed to know that they weren't cheating on me. I would love my dates so much that I would become obsessed. I would dress like them, think like them, listen to the records they enjoyed. I would forget about me! ("Parade" 4, emphasis original)

Like love and pity or desire and identification, sentimentality and psychosis can be hard to distinguish.

The other problem involved his long list of requirements:

Potential boyfriends could not smoke Merit cigarettes, own or wear a pair of cowboy boots, or eat anything labeled either *lite* or *heart smart.* Speech was important, and disqualifying phrases included "I can't find my nipple ring" and "This one here was my *first* tattoo." All street names had to be said in full, meaning no "Fifty-ninth and Lex," and definitely no "Mad Ave." They couldn't drink more than I did, couldn't write poetry in notebooks and read it out loud to an audience of strangers, and couldn't use the words *flick, freebie, cyberspace, progressive,* or *zeitgeist.* They could not consider the human scalp an appropriate palette for self-expression, could not own a rainbow-striped flag, and could not say they had "discovered" any shop or restaurant currently listed in the phone book.

Age, race, and weight were unimportant. As for mutual interests, Sedaris figured they could spend the rest of their lives discussing how much they "hated" the aforementioned characteristics ("See You Again Yesterday" 154, emphasis original).

Hugh presumably met those standards. He mustn't smoke Merits, wear cowboy boots, or eat anything *lite*. He mustn't have tattoos, say "Mad Ave" or *freebie,* drink more than Sedaris, read poetry to strangers, own a rainbow flag, or "discover" restaurants. Another attraction, Hugh's father having worked for the State Department, was a childhood in Africa:

> One of his field trips was literally a trip to a field where the class watched a wrinkled man fill his mouth with rotten goat meat and feed it to a pack of waiting hyenas. On another occasion they were taken to examine the bloodied bedroom curtains hanging in the palace of the former dictator. There were tamer trips, to textile factories and sugar refineries, but my favorite is always the slaughterhouse. It wasn't a big company, just a small rural enterprise run by a couple of brothers operating out of a low-ceilinged concrete building. Following a brief lecture on the importance of proper sanitation, a small white piglet was herded into the room, its dainty hooves clicking against the concrete floor. The class gathered in a circle to get a better look at the animal, who seemed delighted with the attention he was getting. He turned from face to face and was looking up at Hugh when one of the brothers drew a pistol from his back pocket, held it against the animal's temple, and shot the piglet, execution style. Blood spattered, frightened children wept, and the man with the gun offered the teacher and bus driver some meat from a freshly slaughtered goat.

Some people have all the luck, thinks Sedaris. When he was in elementary school, "the best we ever got was a trip to Old Salem or Colonial Williamsburg, one of those preserved brick villages where time supposedly stands still and someone earns his living as a town crier." And also where "[e]very now and then you might come across a doer of bad deeds serving time in the stocks" ("Remembering My Childhood on the Continent of Africa" 192–94). *A doer of bad deeds*—in other words, a target of satire.

Yet another attraction was that Sedaris himself could live abroad:

> Hugh had moved to New York after spending six years in France. I asked a few questions, rightly sensing that he probably wouldn't offer anything unless provoked. There was, he said, a house in Normandy. This was most likely followed by a qualifier, something pivotal like "but it's a dump." He probably described it in detail, but by that point I was only half listening. Instead, I'd begun to imagine my life in a foreign country, some faraway land where, if things went wrong, I could always blame somebody else, saying I'd never wanted to live there in the first place. Life might be difficult for a year or two, but I would tough it out because living in a foreign country is one of those things that everyone should try at least once. My understanding was that it completed a person, sanding down the rough provincial edges and transforming you into a citizen of the world.

Not that he saw this as a "romantic" idea. It had nothing to do with France itself, with "wearing hats or writing tortured letters from a sidewalk café." It had nothing to do with "where Hemingway drank or Alice B. Toklas had her mustache trimmed." What Sedaris did find appealing in

life abroad, though, was "the inevitable sense of helplessness it would inspire." And this being France, there was
also the shopping to consider. (Think wax vagina.) There
was the smoking, too. "And you actually saw people
smoking in restaurants?" he asked. "Really! And offices,
too? Oh, tell me again about the ashtrays in the hospital
waiting room, and don't leave anything out." Even to this
day—despite or perhaps due to her death from lung cancer—Sedaris is next best smoker after Sharon ("See You
Again Yesterday" 154–55, 158).

Hugh doesn't, however, conform to most of the ideals.
He's not straight, of course. He doesn't dislike Sedaris—
unless provoked. And although I'm in no position to know
Hugh's endowment, or if he's a top, I do know—despite
never having seen a photograph—that Sedaris finds him
neither braw nor pulchritudinous. There's the interest in
real estate (Norman dumps, Parisian apartments), which
is "what fortunate couples"—like Lou and Sharon, ostensibly—"turn to when their sex life has faded and they're
too pious for affairs" ("The Ship Shape" 23). There's that
comment in "The Knockout": "I have a boyfriend, who
maybe doesn't look like Hugh but definitely cooks like
him." There's also the conclusion thereof: "If I really can't
sleep, I kill time casting and recasting both my coach and
the genetically altered Hugh" ("The Late Show" 257, 259).
In fact, the only ideals to which Hugh does conform are the
problem ones: he's both intelligent and sentimental.

When the two of them took IQ tests, Hugh scored
"right on the cusp of Mensa qualification." Sedaris, of
course, turned out to be "really stupid, practically an
idiot." The fact that this surprised Sedaris, he quips, "only
bespeaks the depths of my ignorance" ("Smart Guy" 246).
In other words, Hugh's *too* intelligent. Perhaps "fiercely"
so. Perhaps too ironic as well—even though Sedaris either
finds or pretends to find Hugh incapable of irony. At that

fair in Paris, Hugh "unironically characterized the atmosphere as 'carnival-like'" ("I Almost Saw This Girl Get Killed" 233). While vacationing in Slovenia, Hugh—"with no trace of irony"—suggested that the history of the chocolate chip might make for an exciting musical. "If, of course, you found the right choreographer" ("Smart Guy" 244). But irony, as Sedaris knows, isn't sarcasm. It isn't like an on/off switch. It's like a rheostat, a rhetorical dimmer switch that allows for a range of effects between "I almost mean what I say" and "I mean the opposite of what I say." (See Griffin 65–66.) So it may be that Sedaris himself is being ironic when he characterizes Hugh as not so. At least, how else should one understand the end of "Smart Guy"?

> The tests reflected my ability to reason logically. Either you reason things out or you don't. Those who do, have high IQs. Those who don't reach for the mayonnaise when they can't find the insect repellent. When I became upset over my test score, Hugh explained that everybody thinks differently—I just happen to do it a lot less than the average adult.
>
> "Think donkey," he said. "Then take it down a few notches."
>
> It's a point I can't really argue. My brain wants nothing to do with reason. It never has. If I was told to vacate my apartment by next week, I wouldn't ask around or consult the real estate listings. Instead, I'd just imagine myself living in a moated sugar-cube castle, floating from room to room on a king-size magic carpet. If I have one saving grace, it's that I'm lucky enough to have found someone willing to handle the ugly business of day-to-day living.

Hugh consoled me, saying "Don't let it get to you. There are plenty of things you're good at."

When asked for some examples, he listed vacuuming and naming stuffed animals. He says he can probably come up with a few more, but he'll need some time to think. ("Smart Guy" 246–47)

I'd have listed writing—and meant it.

As for sentimentality, here's Hugh having lost it—in more than one sense—at the movies:

One summer evening in Paris, Hugh and I went to see *The End of the Affair,* a Neil Jordan adaptation of the Graham Greene novel. I had trouble keeping my eyes open because I was tired and not completely engaged. Hugh had trouble keeping his eyes open because they were essentially swollen shut: he sobbed from beginning to end, and by the time we left the theater, he was completely dehydrated. I asked if he always cried during comedies, and he accused me of being grossly insensitive, a charge I'm trying to plea-bargain down to simply obnoxious.

Looking back, I should have known better than to accompany Hugh to a love story. Such movies are always a danger, as unlike battling aliens or going undercover to track a serial killer, falling in love is something most adults have actually experienced at some point in their lives. The theme is universal and encourages the viewer to make a number of unhealthy comparisons, ultimately raising the question "Why can't *our* lives be like that?" It's a box best left unopened, and its avoidance explains the continued popularity of vampire epics and martial-arts extravaganzas.

The End of the Affair made me look like an
absolute toad. The movie's voracious couple was
played by Ralph Fiennes and Julianne Moore, who
did everything but eat each other. Their love was
doomed and clandestine, and even when the bombs
were falling, they looked radiant. The picture was
fairly highbrow, so I was surprised when the
director employed a device most often seen in TV
movies of the week: everything's going along just
fine and then one of the characters either coughs or
sneezes, meaning that within twenty minutes he or
she will be dead. It might have been different had
Julianne Moore suddenly started bleeding from
the eyes, but coughing, in and of itself, is fairly
pedestrian. When she did it, Hugh cried. When I
did it, he punched me in the shoulder and told me
to move.

"I don't know if it was their good looks or their passion,"
Sedaris reflects, "but something about Julianne Moore
and Ralph Fiennes put me on the defensive" ("The End of
the Affair" 137–38, emphasis original).

Not that Hugh's romantic anymore—with Sedaris.
He, too, has descended—or perhaps risen—to a Sharon-
like level. Things change, after all, "once you've been
together for more than ten years." That's why they don't
make movies about life partners. "Our lives are boring."
Or maybe not. Here's Hugh having lost it at home:

Hugh and I have been together for so long that in
order to arouse extraordinary passion, we need to
engage in physical combat. Once, he hit me on
the back of the head with a broken wineglass, and
I fell to the floor pretending to be unconscious.
That was romantic, or would have been had he
rushed to my side rather than stepping over my

body to fetch the dustpan. ("The End of the
Affair" 138–39)

I'm sure Hugh was provoked, as when he called Sedaris "a
big, fat, hairy pig" ("Naked" 253).

Despite such scenes, Sedaris figures things will work
themselves out. Otherwise, he doesn't really give their
problems much thought. And if "neither of us would ever
publicly display affection," or "profess love without talking through hand puppets," or even "discuss our relationship"—to Sedaris, that's a "good thing." Those puppets, to
me, are indicated masks ("The End of the Affair" 139).

Another problem is that while Hugh mustn't smoke
Merits, it's also true he doesn't smoke at all. Nor does he
let Sedaris smoke in any room they both currently occupy.
The trouble with such "aggressive nonsmokers," for Sedaris,
is that they feel they're doing you a favor by not allowing
you to smoke. They seem to think that one day you'll look
back and thank them for those precious fifteen seconds
they've just added to your life. "What they don't seem to
understand is that those are just fifteen more seconds you
can spend hating their guts and plotting revenge" ("Diary
of a Smoker" 152).

Another problem is that Hugh's a better a visual artist
than Sedaris. He sculpts, he paints, he's a photographer, a
set designer. This, of course, puts him in the same enviable
category as Gretchen, Tiffany, and, for that matter, Brandi.

Another is that Hugh himself, provoked, can be abusive. In private, either physically or emotionally abusive:
hitting Sedaris with a wineglass, calling him a pig. In public, just emotionally: humiliating Sedaris before dinner
guests—even, alarmingly, when unprovoked. Here's Sedaris
having lost it at home:

> "My boss has a rubber hand," I told our
> Parisian dinner guests following my one and only

day of work. The French word for *boss* is our word
for *chef,* so it sounded even better than I'd expected.
A chef with a rubber hand. You'd think it would
melt.

The guests leaned closer to our table, not sure
if I was using the right word. "Your *chef?* Since
when did you start working?" They turned to Hugh
for confirmation. "He has a job?"

Thinking, I guess, that I wouldn't notice,
Hugh set down his fork and mouthed the words
"It's volunteer work." What irritated me was the
manner in which he said it—not outright, but
barely whispered, the way you might if your
three-year-old was going on about his big day at
school. "It's day care." ("Who's the Chef?" 225,
emphasis original)

You recall the interest in body parts, or representations
thereof. That title, by the way—"Who's the Chef?"—refers
to the Judith Light, Tony Danza sitcom "Who's the Boss?"
(1984–92).

At any rate, the scene got even worse:

"Volunteer or not, I still had a chef," I said.
"And his hand was made of rubber." I'd sat on this
information for hours, had even rehearsed its
delivery, double-checking all the important words
in the dictionary. I don't know what I'd expected—
but it definitely wasn't this.

"I'm sure it wasn't *actual* rubber," Hugh said.
"It was probably some kind of plastic."

The friends agreed, but they hadn't seen my
chef, hadn't watched as he thoughtlessly wedged a
pencil between his man-made fingers. A plastic
hand wouldn't have given quite so easily. A plastic
hand would have made a different sound against

the tabletop. "I know what I saw," I said. "It was
rubber and it smelled like a pencil eraser."

If someone had told me that his boss's hand
smelled like a pencil eraser, I'd shut up and go with
it, but Hugh was in one of his moods. "What, this
guy let you smell his hand?"

"Well, no," I said. "Not exactly."

"Okay, then, it was plastic."

"So, what," I said, "is everything *not* held
directly to your nose made out of plastic? Is that
the rule now?" One of our joint New Year's
resolutions was to stop bickering in front of
company, but he was making it really hard. "The
hand was rubber," I said. "Heavy rubber, like a tire."

Stop bickering in front of company. In other words, "Be
good." But to continue:

"So it was inflatable?" The guests laughed at
Hugh's little joke, and I took a moment to think the
worse of them. An inflatable hand is preposterous
and not worth imagining. Couldn't they see that?

"Look," I said, "this wasn't something I saw in
a shop. I was right there, in the room with it."

"Fine," Hugh said. "So what else?"

"What do you mean, 'what else'?"

"Your volunteer job. So the boss had an
artificial hand—what else?"

Let me explain that it isn't easy finding
volunteer work in Paris. The government pays
people to do just about everything, especially
during an election year, and when I visited the
benevolence center, the only thing available was a
one-day job helping to guide the blind through one
of the city's Metro stations. The program was run
by my chef, who'd set up a temporary office in a

small windowless room beside the ticket booth.
It wasn't my fault that no blind people showed up.
"Listen," I said, "I just spent six hours in a storage
closet being ignored by a man with a rubber hand.
What do you mean, 'What else?' What more do
I need?"

The friends stared blankly, and I realized that
I'd been speaking in English.

"In French," Hugh said. "Say it in French."

It was one of those times when you really notice the difference between speaking and expressing yourself. Sedaris
knew the words—*blind people, election year, storage closet
(les aveugles, l'année des élections, cabinet de débarras)*—
but even when coupled with verbs and pronouns they
didn't add up the way he needed them to. In English,
though, his sentences could perform double duty, "saying
both that I'd reported for volunteer work *and* that Hugh
would be punished for not listening to the single most
interesting thing that had happened to me since moving
to Paris."

"Just forget it," I said.

"Suit yourself."

I left the table for a glass of water, and when
I returned Hugh was discussing Monsieur DiBiasio,
the plumber hired to replace our bathroom sink.

"He's got one arm," I told the guests.

"No, he doesn't," Hugh said. "He's got two."

"Yes, but one of them doesn't work."

"Well, he's still *got* it," Hugh said. "It's *there.*
It fills a sleeve."

He's always doing this, contradicting me in
front of company. And so I did what I always do,
which is ask a question and then deny him a
chance to answer.

"Define *an arm*," I said. "If you're talking
about the long hairy thing that hangs from your
shoulder, okay, he's got two, but if you're talking
about a long hairy thing that moves around and
actually *does* shit then he's got one, all right?
I should know. I'm the one who carried the sink up
three goddam flights of stairs. Me, not you."

The guests were getting uncomfortable, but Sedaris didn't
care. Technically, Hugh was right. The plumber had two
arms. But they weren't in a courtroom, and there was no
punishment for a little exaggeration. People like "mental
pictures." They give them something to do besides just listening. Hadn't they been through this? Instead of backing
him up, Hugh made Sedaris out to be a liar—as Monie
had—"and, oh, I hated him for that" ("Who's the Chef?"
226–28, emphasis original).

Other such "mental pictures," by the way, have been
provided by Lisa ("It provoked a startling mental picture,
capturing a moment in time when one's actions seem both
unimaginably cruel and completely natural" ["Repeat After
Me" 154]), by Sharon ("It was hard to shake the mental
picture snapped by her suggestion: here is a boy sitting on
a bed, his mouth smeared with chocolate. He's a human
being, but also he's a pig, surrounded by trash and gorging himself so that others may be denied" ["Us and Them"
12]), and by Hugh himself—provoked (*"Big* is something
I can live with. *Fat* is open to interpretation, but when
coupled with the word *hairy,* it begins to form a mental
picture that is brought into sharp focus when united with
the word *pig*. A big, fat, hairy pig" ["Naked" 253]). They've
not been, however, by Julian. "I wanted a good mental picture of what it might be like with three or four studs at
one time," writes Chad, "ramming away and taking it all"
("My Manuscript" 30).

Why provoke, though? Why abuse, presumably, or be an asshole? Maybe to punish Hugh for being smart or too good an artist—more envy-based but not just imagined inhumanity. Maybe to punish him for being gay or kind. For not being—or playing—some ideal straight guy. Or some "daddy." Most partners, however, play multiple roles—as do writers with readers. We—as partners—play both husband and wife *and* parent and child. Or parent and infant: "He said it the way you might if your three-year-old was going on about his big day at school." We play both teacher-and-student *and* master-and-slave. Or master-and-servant. Both brother-and-sister and uncle-and-niece. Or brother-and-brother, uncle-and-nephew. Both doctor-and-patient and patient-and-nurse. Or doctor-and-nurse. Both Santa-and-Elf and Judith-and-Tony. Or both Judith-and-Tony and Sharon-and-Lou. If lucky, of course, we're also friends. Real ones, as are Sedaris and Hugh: "I picked up the next [Emmy], moving on to Hugh, Evelyne, Ira, Susan, Jim, Ronnie, Marge, and Steve" ("The Curly Kind" 166).

Of course some such roles, parent-and-infant in particular, are inappropriate—as when Sedaris played friend to Sharon or, worse, father to either Tiffany or Paul. Some, moreover, are incompatible, resulting in no-win situations from which it's hard to extricate yourself. You're *goddamned* if you do, as in Hugh's case ("I'm the one who carried the sink up three goddam flights of stairs"), but also—more important—goddamned if he doesn't. Sedaris, for example, identifies with Sharon. There's introjection too. Hugh, then, should impersonate Lou, or abusive husband. ("I wound up in Normandy the same way my mother wound up in North Carolina," Sedaris figures: "you meet a guy, relinquish a tiny bit of control, and the next thing you know, you're eating a different part of the pig" ["See You Again Yesterday" 153].) So some provocations, never specified, may constitute both punishment for not doing this and attempts to make him—to make Hugh, in turn, use shame abusively. And given who Lou really is, to Sedaris, Hugh should also impersonate not just some daddy but that particular one. But given his own needs, identifications, and introjections—whatever they are—not to mention the cooking and baking, this may be something Hugh can't do. At any rate, Sedaris himself identifies with Lou— as both Tiffany and Paul can attest. (No introjection, though. The man's alive.) Any son would, even—or especially—an abused one. Hugh, then, should also—somehow—impersonate Sharon, or abused wife. So some provocations may both constitute punishment for not doing that and an attempt to make him. And given who she really was, to Sedaris—given, too, that Sedaris may need a partner to replace her—Hugh should also impersonate Sharon as nurturing mother. So some provocations may constitute attempts to make him, in turn, use shame *non*-abusively. But this too, given Hugh's needs, identifications, and introjections, not to mention the sentimentality and aversion to cigarettes, may be something he can't.

Proust himself never knew such multiple role playing. For one thing, he imagined lovers in individual roles: Reynaldo Hahn was just a friend; Lucien Daudet, a brother; Bertrand de Fénelon, a "siren"; Alfred Agostinelli— his mechanic, then secretary—a "nun." (See Tadié 238, 240, 387, 499.) For another, no such coupling survived the end of the affair. And so even the two longest and, arguably, most successful relationships in *Remembrance of Things Past* fail to feature it. Or rather, the multiple role playing they do feature is sequential. Those lovers then life partners play role after role, but never more than one at a time. No true multiplicity, and so no incompatibility. Mlle Vinteuil and her unnamed friend, for example, are first posited as brother and sister, then as two brothers, and then two sisters, and finally as two mothers—mothers, moreover, both entirely and selflessly devoted to one another. (See Ladenson 98.) Baron de Charlus and Jupien, a tailor, are first posited as master and servant. (But in a hint of true multiplicity—and possible incompatibility— it's the socially inferior Jupien who may be the sexual boss. "What a big ass you have," he tells Charlus the day they meet—at about the age of Sedaris today: "All right, you big baby, come along!" [4: 13]. For Sedgwick, the relationship now begun "is demonstrated—though it is never stated—to be the single exception to every Proustian law of desire, jealousy, triangulation, and radical epistemological instability; without any comment or rationalization, Jupien's love of Charlus is shown to be steadfast over decades and grounded in a completely secure knowledge of a fellow-creature who is neither his opposite nor his simulacrum" [220].) In the end though—our final Proust— they're just mother and son:

> The cab turned into the Champs-Elysées and, as I did not particularly want to hear the whole of the concert which was being given at the Guermantes party, I stopped it and was preparing to get out in order to walk a few yards when I was struck by the spectacle presented by another cab which was also stopping. A man with staring eyes and hunched figure was placed rather than seated in the back, and was making, to keep himself upright, the efforts that might have been made by a child who has been told to be good. But his straw hat failed to conceal an unruly forest of hair which was entirely white, and a white beard, like those which snow forms on the statues of river-gods in public gardens, flowed from his chin. It was—side by side with Jupien, who was unremitting in his

attentions to him—M. de Charlus, now convalescent
after an attack of apoplexy of which I had had no
knowledge (I had only been told that he had lost
his sight, but in fact this trouble had been purely
temporary and he could now see quite well again)
and which, unless the truth was that hitherto he
had dyed his hair and that he had now been
forbidden to continue so fatiguing a practice, had
had the effect, as in a sort of chemical precipitation,
of rendering visible and brilliant all that saturation
of metal which the locks of his hair and his beard,
pure silver now, shot forth like so many geysers, so
that upon the old fallen prince this latest illness
had conferred the Shakespearian majesty of a King
Lear. His eyes had not remained unaffected by this
total convulsion, this metallurgical transformation
of his head, but had, by an inverse phenomenon,
lost all their brightness. But what was most moving
was that one felt that this lost brightness was
identical with his moral pride, and that somehow
the physical and even the intellectual life of
M. de Charlus had survived the eclipse of that
aristocratic haughtiness which had in the past
seemed indissolubly linked to them. To confirm this,
at the moment which I am describing, there passed
in a victoria, no doubt also on her way to the
reception of the Prince de Guermantes, Mme de
Saint-Euverte, whom formerly the Baron had not
considered elegant enough for him. Jupien, who
tended him like a child, whispered in his ear that it
was someone with whom he was acquainted, Mme
de Saint-Euverte. And immediately, with infinite
laboriousness but with all the concentration of a
sick man determined to show that he is capable of
all the movements which are still difficult for him,

M. de Charlus lifted his hat, bowed, and greeted
Mme de Saint-Euverte as respectfully as if she had
been the Queen of France or as if he had been a
small child coming timidly in obedience to his
mother's command to say "How do you do?" to a
grown-up person. For a child, but without a child's
pride, was what he had once more become. Perhaps
the very difficulty that M. de Charlus had in
making these gestures was in itself a reason for
him to make them, in the knowledge that he would
create a greater effect by an action which, painful
for an invalid, became thereby doubly meritorious
on the part of the man who performed it and
doubly flattering to the individual to whom it
was addressed, invalids, like kings, practicing
exaggerated civility. Perhaps also there was in the
movements of the Baron that lack of co-ordination
which follows upon maladies of the spinal column
and the brain, so that his gestures went beyond
anything that he intended. What I myself saw in
them was above all a sort of gentleness, an almost
physical gentleness, and of detachment from the
realities of life, phenomena so strikingly apparent
in those whom death has already drawn within its
shadow. And exposure of the veins of silver in his
hair was less indicative of profound alterations
than this unconscious humility which turned all
social relations upside down and abased before
Mme de Saint-Euverte—as it would have abased
before the most vulgar of American hostesses
(who at last would have been able to congratulate
herself on the hitherto unattainable politeness of
the Baron)—what had seemed to be the proudest
snobbishness of all. For the Baron still lived, still
thought; his intellect was not impaired. And more

than any chorus of Sophocles on the humbled
pride of Oedipus, more than death itself or any
funeral oration on the subject of death, the humble
greeting, full of effort to please, which the Baron
addressed to Mme de Saint-Euverte proclaimed
the fragile and perishable nature of the love of
earthly greatness and all human pride. M. de
Charlus, who until this moment would never have
consented to dine with Mme de Saint-Euverte,
now bowed to the ground in her honor. To receive
the homage of M. de Charlus had been, for her,
the highest ambition of snobbery, just as, for the
Baron, the central principle of snobbery had been
to be rude to her. And now this inaccessible and
precious essence which he had succeeded in
making Mme de Saint-Euverte believe to be
part of his nature, had at a single stroke been
annihilated by M. de Charlus, by the earnest
timidity, the apprehensive zeal with which he
raised a hat from beneath which, all the while that
his head remained deferentially uncovered, there
streamed with the eloquence of a Bossuet the
torrents of his silvery hair. Jupien helped the
Baron to descend and I greeted him. He spoke to
me very rapidly, in a voice so inaudible that I could
not distinguish what he was saying, which wrung
from him, when for the third time I made him
repeat his remarks, a gesture of impatience that
astonished me by its contrast with the impassivity
which his face had at first displayed, which was no
doubt an after-effect of his stroke. But when after
a while I had grown accustomed to this pianissimo
of whispered words, I perceived that the sick man
retained the use of his intelligence absolutely
intact. (6: 244–47)

Of course it's hard to imagine Sedaris and Hugh, like Vinteuil and friend, ever mothering one another. Just as we don't know Sedaris the man, we know even less about Hugh—or, once again, about his needs, identifications, and introjections. But it's easy to imagine "Sedaris" alone, years from now, as Jupien. Call it, if not another "spectacle," a mental picture.

[Your Name Here]

The *Maxims* of La Rochefoucauld, or rather "La Roche-foucauld," are primarily addressed to a friend of his: Mme de La Fayette (1634–93), author of the first great novel in French (*The Princesse de Clèves* [1678]). *Remembrance of Things Past,* perhaps the last one, may be addressed: (1) to Proust himself (this novel, according to Walter Benjamin, combines "an unparalleled intensity of conversation with an unsurpassable aloofness" [212]); (2) to Proust's mother ("Is it not the mother," asks Eve Sedgwick, "to whom both the coming-out testament and its continued refusal to come out are addressed?" [248]); or (3) to no one in particular (every reader, says Gérard Genette, "knows himself to be the implied—and anxiously awaited—narratee of this swirling narrative" [261]). Roland Barthes would—but can't—address a lover: "To know that one does not write for the other, to know that these things I am going to write will never cause me to be loved by the one I love (the other), to know that writing compensates for nothing, sublimates nothing, that it is precisely *there where you are not*—this is the beginning of writing" (*A Lover's Discourse* 100, emphasis original). So he settles for cruising. (See Kopelson 129–50.) Of course, like any writer—or like either Nietzsche in class or men Sedaris finds unacceptable—they're also addressing an "audience of strangers." (Nietzsche: "Will he not be obliged to speak before an audience of strangers of things which he can safely speak of only amongst his nearest friends?" [*Untimely Meditations* 186]. Sedaris: "They couldn't drink more than I did, couldn't write poetry in notebooks and read it out loud to an audience of strangers" ["See You Again Yesterday" 154].) They're also, that is, addressing you.

As for Sedaris, we've seen him address: (1) Sharon; (2) Lou; (3) Paul; (4) Madelyn; (5) both Lisa and Tiffany, by way of apology; (6) people like that brat by the elevator, by way of both nurturing shame and instruction; (7) people like that asshole with the jade, by way of abuse; and (8) anyone who identifies with such brats or assholes. But whereas Sedaris speaks to both Sharon and his sisters in more or less his own voice—as "Sedaris"—he speaks to such brats, by and large, as Sharon and to such assholes, as Lou: sanguine for the former, cynical for the latter. How, then, does he speak to the rest of us—including readers who identify with such brats and assholes? How address—in prose—his own audience of strangers? We know—because we're told so—that he considers us American. ("It doesn't interest me to manipulate the French. I'm not keyed in to their value system. Because they are not my people, their imagined praise or condemnation means nothing to me. Paris, it seems, is where I've come to dream about America" ["The Late Show" 263].) But we also know he considers us children. Beloved children, that is, and Sharon's in particular. In fact, he considers us Sedaris himself. And so the typical "Sedaris"

essay, or story, impersonates Sharon mothering the son
doing that very impersonation.

This, in addition to the autobiography or confession,
is what's so unusual about Sedaris. And it's one reason
we love him. Or love him back. (Best-Loved Uncle? I say,
Best-Loved Satirist.) Another reason concerns both autobiography and self-deprecation. Satire has been accused
of failing to disturb most readers, who rarely see themselves as targets. "Satire is a sort of glass," writes Jon-
athan Swift (1667–1745), "wherein beholders do generally
discover everybody's face but their own; which is the chief
reason for that kind of reception it meets in the world, and
that so very few are offended with it." Sedaris, however, is
a mirror in which "Sedaris" himself—for the most part—
is reflected: (1) someone we feel we come to know, as a
friend (entertaining but also challenging us); (2) someone
we do come to love, as either mother or father (an affective
investment that enables nurturing shame to do the trick,
in the privacy of our own reading experience—and so
"these things," to paraphrase Barthes, cause Sedaris to
be loved by those he himself seems to love); (3) someone
we love without having to say so, or say so back (antisentimental Sedaris, in effect, never demands an *I love
you, too*—he simply nurtures); and (4) someone we pity as
well, for having lost Sharon. But he's also someone—or
rather, someone else—with whom we identify. Apart, that
is, from those brats and assholes. I mean, apart from those
other ones. Because while to love Sedaris is in a sense
to love ourselves, it's also to hate—no, not ourselves. It's
to hate not the foolish but the vicious or inhumane things
we either do, can imagine doing, or can imagine having
been done by someone else. It's to follow Sharon's instruction—to take a good look at Sedaris *as* ourselves, turn
"our hatred inward," and then feel we can improve ("Us
and Them" 12).

Of course, I'm not saying that's the only role-playing here. Readers posited as Child Sedaris—to be shamed in maternal or instructed in pedagogical fashion—are also posited, as suggested above, as Father Lou, Mother Sharon, Sister, Brother, Teacher, Friend, Coworker, Niece or Nephew (Madelyn or "Marty"), and Partner Hugh. Or even as Customer. ("Don't tell the store president I called you a bitch. Tell him I called you a fucking bitch, because that's exactly what you are. Now get out of my sight before I do something we both regret" ["SantaLand Diaries" 196].) But only intermittently, and rarely with the same intensity. So, unlike Hugh, we never find ourselves in no-win situations.

Or almost never. Take "Giantess" and "After Malison," both of which posit readers—primarily—as customers. *Sedaris* customers. In "Giantess," he chronicles a decision not to write for the eponymous publication, erotica addressed to men a bit too mother-minded:

> My sister [Amy?] once gave me a magazine
> called *Knocked Up and Gun Toting,* which featured
> nude, pregnant women sporting firearms: pistols,
> hunting rifles, Uzis—you name it. I don't imagine
> *Knocked Up and Gun Toting* has a very wide
> circulation but I'm certain its subscribers are
> devoted and happy in their own way. Still, though,
> like with *Giantess,* I have a hard time sharing
> their fetish. I shudder at the thought of nipples the
> size of manhole covers. Beneath the surface the
> *Giantess* reader seems to be a man who longs for
> infancy. He looks back fondly at the time he was
> dwarfed by his mother and scolded for soiling
> himself. And that's just about the last experience
> I care to reflect upon. Sure I received a few
> spankings but I never considered them a high

point. I moved on and got on with my life. Didn't I?
("Giantess" 159–60)

Didn't *we,* that is? What's the difference, really, between
having been "scolded" and having been shamed? What's
the difference between *Giantess* the magazine and "Giantess" the essay?

   "After Malison" is fiction, and hence—perhaps—even
more truthful. In it, however, the author "Malison" doesn't
represent the story's author. For all we know, moreover, he
doesn't even represent *Malison.* Both snobbish and arro-
gant—not to mention assholic—he's more evil twin than
alter ego, more Bergotte than Buddy Glass. (Whereas
people like Sedaris, for example, are written off, by the
narrator, as "fussy, middle-of-the-road contemporaries,"
Malison—a character based, in part, on Charles Bukowski
[1920–1994]—creates postmodern metafiction with titles
like *Rotunda Surf, Magnetic Plugs,* and *Smithy Smithy. Rotunda Surf* begins: "If you, reader, can yank your head out
of your asshole long enough to finish the first chapter, don't
make the mistake of congratulating yourself. You possess
nothing but fleeting, momentary courage. The shit on your
face is still wet. It is your mask." In *Smithy Smithy,* every
character is named Smithy Smithy. And the "whole point"
of such work, says the narrator, is that "hardly anyone"—
except for Malison—"is a wonderful person" [119–20].) So
he's easy to distinguish from Sedaris. But it's hard—in fact,
it's impossible—to distinguish Anastasia, that narrator,
from the story's reader. From oneself, that is. Equally assholic—or *bitchy*—Anastasia is Malison's most appreciative
fan. Or so she'd have it. She's a stalker as well. Here she
is, in what may or may not be Malison's hotel but what's
definitely—on the part of Sedaris—an allusion to Swift:

   I'm sitting in the cocktail lounge of The
Chesterton, a grotesque, brassy place ironically

named Reflections, which erroneously suggests that I will see myself mirrored in this bar or any of its customers. I sit at a table, pull out my journal, and, when the waitress arrives, I order a boilermaker. The waitress acts shocked that a woman might order a beer and a shot rather than some frozen daiquiri product, and I shoot her a look that sends her off toward a group of people she thinks might find her cute.

Malison's reading is starting right at this moment, I can sense it. I think it's very appropriate, very revealing that right now he is standing before an audience of people who don't understand him, and at the same time I'm sitting in this bar full of people who, I am certain, have no hope of ever knowing or understanding me. It's a lonely feeling, but I'd rather be alone than stoop to a lower level of understanding. The waitress brings me my shot and my beer and gives me a look while I empty the shot glass into the beer. She acts as though I'm spoiling all her fun. Whatever fun she might have working in a place like this, leading her dull, unexamined life, she is more than welcome to. She can have it. The customers are all looking at me the same way. They can't deal with anyone who isn't into their Mr. and Mrs. Jovial scene, with someone who takes a hard look at the crumbling building blocks that are the foundations for their wasted suburban lives. With someone like me.

This place reminds me of the bar that Malison depicted in *Magnetic Plugs,* except the people are fully dressed and they're not drinking out of gas cans. The waitress returns and I order another boilermaker. ("After Malison" 117–18)

Wouldn't we all? Order another, that is.

"After Malison," then, is a looking glass in which you can't not find—no, not Sedaris. In which you can't not find your own face. Like "Giantess," moreover, reading it puts you in a no-win situation. Because like anything by Sedaris, you can't not love it. And you can't love it, or him, without also—despite Anastasia's example—going after *Sedaris.* Not that I, too, am a stalker, or anything else that bad. But I can imagine it.

Literary Interpolations

André

What, if anything, is Gide doing in *The Immoralist* (1921)—to himself as well as to the reader—that the narrator, his alter ego "Michel," couldn't be doing alone were his a true confession? What, that is, other than "stating a problem," to cite the author's somewhat disingenuous preface (xiv). Michel, ostensibly, is asking his friends for help, but doesn't really seem to want it. His friends, for their part, want to help—in fact, they're duty bound to do so—but also feel that Michel's confession has legitimized his actions, turning them, the friends, into unwilling "accomplices," and that they can't condemn him for two transgressions moralists find reprehensible: fooling around with pretty boys and letting his wife, Marceline, die (169).

True confessions, on the one hand, are abject speech acts in which one assumes theologically, juridically, and psychoanalytically transgressive subject positions: sinner, criminal, pervert, and so on. They needn't be read symptomatically, excepting the psychoanalytic context. They needn't be public, excepting the Protestant one. They're monological, to cite Bakhtin. They're true, presumably—but for the possibility that all such identity formation involves false consciousness or misrecognition. And along with identity formation, true confessions—within these institutional contexts—compel condemnation, absolution, conviction, or cure. Within noninstitutional contexts these speech acts may compel analogous responses (condemnation, forgiveness, help), but also, and more clearly, require some sort of emotion—or affect—on the part of both interlocutors: love, pity, even anger. (Love and pity are emotions; anger, an affect.)

Literary confessions, on the other hand, play with, and against, all these rules of formation. And they almost always require symptomatic reading. The *récit* form, in particular, is profoundly ironic; Michel, for example, doesn't recognize, as we do, just why he finds boys pretty, or enjoys watching them steal. Such confessions may even demand such a reading. Buddy Glass, J. D. Salinger's alter ego in *Seymour: An Introduction* (1959), warns us that a confessional passage has probably never been written that didn't "stink" a little bit of the writer's pride in having given up his pride: "The thing to listen for, every time, with a public confessor, is what he's *not* confessing to" (195, emphasis original). (Buddy, nonetheless, calls himself a "snob" [242].) Literary confessions, moreover, are inherently public. According to de Man, all literary confessors—Rousseau in particular—seek "a stage on which to parade [their] disgrace" (286). They're dialogical, to cite Bakhtin. Yourcenar's anti-Gidean *Alexis* (1929)—a private, monological *récit* in which a married homosexual, instead of killing her as Michel does, both apologizes and explains to his wife why they must separate—is therefore anomalous. They problematize truth. And they oppose institutional pressure. In other words, writers like Gide tend to be rebellious—or like Amy, perverse—and to either transform or transvalue transgression.

Consider *The Kreutzer Sonata* (1889). In it, Tolstoy's wife murderer—a jealous cuckold named Pozdnyshev—ultimately requests forgiveness of his listener, a traveling companion who transmits the murderer's long, analytical confession to us. The listener seems to oblige, touching him with his hand—a gesture of absolution—and feeling both pity and sorrow. We, however, understand such forgiveness to be irrelevant. The true point is that male sexual violence is a product of patriarchy, and that patriarchy itself—not Pozdnyshev—is to blame. (See Kramer 177–79.) Which makes us angry—at patriarchy. Guilt-ridden Pozdnyshev doesn't quite get this: he demands the narrator's forgiveness both because the judicial system has failed to punish him and because he can't forgive himself. Neither does the narrator—Tolstoy's alter ego—seem to get it.

Is Gide's point, then, that what we now call *heteronormativity* is to blame for Marceline's death? Possibly, which may have been what made Yourcenar angry—at Gide.

Or consider *De Profundis* (1897), a confession I don't consider true. In it, Wilde—Ménalque of *The Immoralist*—manages: (1) to pretend to write his own confession; (2) to really write the confession of the pretty boy who landed him in jail, Lord Alfred Douglas; (3) to pretend to forgive Douglas for having done so; (4) to prevent us—now too angry at Douglas for any such generosity of spirit—from forgiving him as well; and (5) to satirize Douglas as selfish. Wilde's speech act is therefore doubly vicarious: the victim does the victimizer's confessing for him, the reader does the writer's feeling.

Is Gide's point, then, to prevent us from forgiving Michel—or at least from becoming his accomplices too?

Possibly. I've no doubt Yourcenar was angry at both Gide and Michel. On the other hand, it's hard to imagine Gide as angry at Michel. If he was secretly angry at any character, it would have been at his alter ego's wife—which would help explain both why he made Marceline so virtuous and why he lets her die.

Or consider *Confessions of Zeno* (1923). Italo Svevo's anti-Freudian alter ego isn't exactly transgressive, although he does betray his wife. Nor, although he thinks of himself as one, is Zeno much of a victim. What Zeno really feels compelled to confess—compelled, that is, by the forsaken psychoanalyst Zeno believes incapable of curing him, and who supposedly publishes the confession in order to "annoy" (i.e., punish) Zeno—is that he's a failure (vii). He's a failure as a husband, as a lover, as a friend, and as a son. Most amusingly, he's also—like both Sharon and Sedaris—a failure at quitting cigarettes. But even though Zeno never manages not to smoke, he does succeed in life. Not, however, because the confession per se ever does any good. (For Svevo, there may never be anything—no truth—to confess; and even if there were, confessional writing, in and of itself, may never be therapeutic.) And not because Dr. S. ever does any good; in fact, no authority figure does. (For Svevo, there is never any cure within the work of psychoanalysis, only punishment.) Ironically enough, Zeno succeeds because, without really trying, he eventually succeeds at business. The irony, of course, is at the doctor's expense; we now know to take Zeno at his word.

Is Gide's point, then, that Michel's friends couldn't help him—as opposed to condemn him—even if they hadn't become accomplices? Or that no one duty bound to help such a confessor (institution or no institution) can ever really help? In other words, is it that no one socially positioned to do good—or *be* good, to cite Sedaris as Adolph—is ever in a good position to do so? Or is it that if help ever does come, it won't have been because Michel—even assuming he does want it—happened to have called for it.

Now, finally, consider *Lolita* (1955). Humbert Humbert addresses both Lolita (admitting that although he did rob her of a childhood, he does love her) and the jury called upon to pronounce him guilty of murdering Quilty (admitting that although he did kill or, rather, execute the man—more alter ego than rival, really—he, Humbert, must have been insane at the time). In addition, he tells the jury about Lolita, and Lolita about the murder. And he seems to want a wide range of self-contradictory "performative" responses from all these listeners: one of them—the jury—institutional and public; the other—Lolita—noninstitutional and private. He wants conviction, acquittal, condemnation, forgiveness—and above all, understanding. (By *performative,* of course, I don't mean theatrical. I mean speech acts that both say and *do* things.) As for affect or emotion, he wants their/her (especially her) anger, pity, and, above all, love. (Needless to say, like Zeno, he also wants to amuse.) Vladimir Nabokov also seems to want all these things from us. But what does he—Humbert—want from himself? What is he trying to do to himself? Like Svevo—or Zeno—he doesn't consider confessional writing especially therapeutic—at least, not in the sense of curative. He considers it, at best, a work of art, which for him means not "beauty plus pity," which is how Nabokov defined art in relation to Kafka's "The Metamorphosis," but something more specific: "I see nothing for the treatment of my misery but the melancholy and very local palliative of articulate art" (285). (So much for amusing himself.) *Palliative,* of course, is an interesting word. It means either an extenuating representation (consider the way Wilde excuses himself), or that which alleviates pain without eliminating disease (consider the temporary relief Pozdnyshev affords himself—no doubt, he'll be telling his tale to other strangers on the train). In other words, *palliative* means that which performs something true confessions, according to their rules of formation, aren't really supposed to, but something even they often do. Something *peri*-performative, to cite Eve Kosofsky Sedgwick.

The Immoralist—like *Remembrance of Things Past*—is another such work of art. Michel, too, and probably Gide as well, sees nothing for the treatment of his misery but the melancholy and very local palliative of articulate art, which is another reason—the main one—why he doesn't really seem to want help. The same, of course, could be said of Proust. As such, both novels tell us not only about the homosexuality of yesteryear, but about the performative—and *peri*-performative—nature of all confession. As for whether *Barrel Fever, Naked, Holidays on Ice, Me Talk Pretty One Day,* and *Dress Your Family in Corduroy and Denim* do more or less the same thing, it's hard to say. Sedaris may be miserable, but he's not *that* miserable—which, of course, tells us something else about gay sexuality.

Eve

Having demonized Lytton Strachey in *The Voyage Out* (1915) by making the purportedly straight character based on Strachey misogynist, Virginia Woolf treats him rather well in *Jacob's Room* (1922). Not only is Richard Bonamy, the decidedly gay character based on Strachey, not misogynist, he's the hero's fondest friend, just as Strachey himself had been to Virginia's brother Thoby. He's also someone with whom Woolf seems to identify: it's Bonamy, after all, who's left alone with Jacob's mother in that suddenly empty room and to whom, holding out a pair of shoes, she poses that suddenly sentimental—unanswerable—question: "What am I to do with these . . . ?" (155). (*This* author identifies with both Woolf and Strachey—because she lost an idealized brother as well as a parent; he, a lover—and hence with Bonamy as well.) Or at least I find the question sentimental, almost unbearably so—which for me (if not for someone like David's mother) happens to be a good thing, and which is why I cherish it more than any other finale in prose fiction.

Yet for Woolf, Bonamy himself, if not Strachey himself, is almost unbearably sentimental—a *bad* thing to be. Sentimentality, according to the momentarily ironic narrator, may be one of the things (along with "blankness of mind" and "haphazard ways") that make "every woman ... nicer than any man" (7), but it's also something of which gay—or stereotypically effeminate—men like Bonamy can be accused. For example, when Bonamy, idealizing Jacob, thinks him "more sublime, devastating, terrific than ever," Woolf remarks without any irony I can detect directed toward her own idealization of Thoby:

> What superlatives! What adjectives! How acquit Bonamy of sentimentality of the grossest sort; of being tossed like a cork on the waves; of having no steady insight into character; of being unsupported by reason, and of drawing no comfort whatever from the works of the classics? (144)

One boring word for this maneuver (far more boring than "identification") might, of course, be projection, and one description of that finale might be the return of the repressed. Woolf tries to dissociate herself from both Victorian femininity and Victorian (if not Edwardian) fiction by attributing the debased sentimentality she finds they share to an effeminate (if not Victorian) associate, but can't help being sentimental herself when touching upon—and hence touched by—the hero's death. (Jacob died in battle; Thoby, of typhus.) Fortunately, there are—there *have* been—other, more interesting words, and other descriptions.

What else, for someone like Woolf (a category that does include both Strachey and—nowadays—Sedaris), is wrong with sentimentality? Apart from being feminine, old-fashioned, and irrational ("unsupported by reason"), it's excessive and insincere. Too much emotion: giving a

thing more tenderness than God does, to cite R. H. Blyth—
or more familiarly, J. D. Salinger. Inauthentic emotion:
as if one could turn such feelings off and on, like charm.
Or like sarcasm. Sentimentality is also, nowadays, and
for presumably homophobic people opposed to Woolf and
Strachey, excessively—almost exclusively—homoerotic.
"Whereas in the nineteenth century it was images of
women in relation to domestic suffering and death that
occupied the most potent, symptomatic, and, perhaps,
friable or volatile place in the sentimental *imaginaire* of
middle-class culture," according to Eve Kosofsky Sedgwick,
"for the succeeding century—the century inaugurated by
Wilde among others—it has been images of agonistic male
self-constitution" (147). Images like Dorian Gray, a sexy
suicide; and maybe even Jacob Flanders.

Woolf's characterization of Strachey, through Bonamy,
as sentimental wasn't exactly inaccurate, but it wasn't
very accurate either. Strachey's biographical writing now
strikes us, as does most Modernist literature, as radi-
cally antisentimental. He favors innuendo and irony (not
sarcasm), caricature and pastiche. He has a "virtuoso"
style, according to his own biographer, "with its ornate
overstatements, its laconic recording of incongruities, its
unpredictable transpositions, its ironic crescendoes and
plummetings into bathos" (Holroyd 428)—much like Sedgwick, perhaps. Some contemporaries did see sentimentality there. Bertrand Russell, reading *Eminent Victorians*
(1918) in Brixton gaol, found "it caused me to laugh so loud
that the officer came to my cell, saying I must remember
that prison is a place for punishment." But Russell de-
tected "girls' school sentimentality" as well (Holroyd 69).
(One recalls, along with Sedgwick, both Wilde's joke on
Dickens ["Must one have a heart of stone to read the
death of Little Nell without laughing?"] and Gore Vidal's
on Wilde ["Must one have a heart of stone to read *The*

Ballad of Reading Gaol without laughing?"]. Sedgwick comments: "If the joke were that the Wilde who took advantage of the enormous rhetorical charge to be gained from hurling at Dickens the aspersion of sentimentality also at another time, perhaps later in his life when the hideous engines of state punishment had done their work of destroying the truth and gaiety of his sensibility, developed a proneness to the same awful failing, that would be one thing. Perhaps, though, the point is that there isn't a differentiation to be *made* between sentimentality and its denunciation. But then we are dealing with a joke that can only be on Gore Vidal himself, whose hypervigilance for lapses in the tough-mindedness of others can then only suggest that he in turn must be, as they say, insecure about his own. It may be only those who are themselves prone to these vicariating impulses who are equipped to detect them in the writing or being of others; but it is they who for several reasons tend therefore to be perturbed in their presence" [153, emphasis original].) Ivor Brown, reading *Queen Victoria* (1921), discovered that the "cool and unsparing portrayer of the Victorian notables was no longer the aloof scrutineer." Following the queen down the decades, he found himself "at last engaged in a sentimental journey"—which for Brown happens to have been a good thing (Holroyd 495). Even Strachey admitted, "I think perhaps my whole treatment of [Cardinal] Newman [in *Eminent Victorians*] is over-sentimentalized—to make a foil for the other Cardinal" (Holroyd 423). Woolf, however, wasn't another such contemporary. She saw no over-sentimentality in the writing—the *public* writing.

But she did see it in Strachey himself—in the man's very "being," to cite Sedgwick, if not in his private correspondence as well. He was too sentimental about crusty old men like Edmund Gosse, and far too sentimental about callow young men like Roger Senhouse—views shared by numerous friends as well as by Strachey. Russell, for example, found that Strachey degraded fellow Apostle G. E. Moore's ethics into "advocacy of a stuffy girls'-school sentimentalizing"—a false charge, according to fellow homosexual E. M. Forster (Holroyd xix). Duncan Grant, that Bloomsbury heartthrob, made him feel "cloudy, I fear almost sentimental," as a love-struck Strachey put it to—of all people—John Maynard Keynes (Holroyd 115). (Keynes, of course, was to alienate Grant's affection.) For some reason, though, the death—in battle—of war poet Rupert Brooke, another such heartthrob, left him cold.

Like Woolf, Strachey was quick to disparage other men's sentimentality, if not to "project" his own onto them. But his reasons differed. Early in life, he'd been impatient with fellow Apostle Goldsworthy Lowes Dickinson, who used sentimentality to *conceal* homosexuality. (Strachey—like Proust in life—was relatively "out.") He later complained—to Dora Carrington, of all people—that Sebastian Sprott, a "charming" young man with whom he'd been traveling ("most easy to get on with, most considerate, very gay, and interested in everything that occurs"), is "inclined to be sentimental, though too clever to be so in a sickly style"—a complaint that must have been generated by the fact that "[h]is sentimentality is not directed towards me" (Holroyd 515). Sprott was Keynes's lover at the time.

Strachey also disparaged—yet unlike Woolf clearly identified with—other women's sentimentality. His Florence Nightingale, in *Eminent Victorians,* ends her days "indulging in sentimental friendships with young girls" and weeping—in print—over old probationers, which may explain Russell's negative reaction (200). His Victoria ends the "sentimental journey" Brown relished in similar ways. All of which may explain Strachey's explicit identification with Bonamy. "I am such a Bonamy," he is said to have remarked upon reading *Jacob's Room* for the first

time. (Given the tough-minded *accusation* of sentimentality, "*Mea culpa*" would have been more appropriate.) The
novel may not involve the character's, *his* character's feelings for suicidal young women, or even for crusty old men,
but it does involve emotions far more central to his, to
our sentimental *imaginaire:* Bonamy's barely sublimated
sexual feelings for a young male friend and would-be
lover, now dying (like Sedgwick), now—finally—dead. And
whereas Strachey may not have been so naive—so bold,
rather—as to have said, or written, that Thoby was "more
sublime, devastating, terrific than ever," he didn't have to
be. Bonamy said, *Woolf* said it for him.

Apart from *Jacob's Room,* with its surprising finale,
and apart from *The Waves* (1931), with its fleeting indica-
tion of yet another lovelorn homosexual, I don't see Woolf
as a sentimental novelist. The death of Rachel Vinrace
in *The Voyage Out* leaves me cold, as it seems to have left
the author. So does the suicide of Septimus Smith in *Mrs.
Dalloway* (1925). I do, however, find Woolf sentimental in
her very "being"—to the extent I can know it at all. (I only
know "Virginia Woolf.") I also find her closet sentimentality feminocentric, and hence too passé for Modernism.
Notwithstanding the slighting of forsaken Fanny Elmer
(Jacob's sweetheart), it was suicidal young women—Carrington in particular—and not doomed young men who
really tugged at Woolf's heartstrings, perhaps because they
shared both a gender and a death wish—as opposed to, say,
a terminal illness. As Ralph Partridge told Gerald Brenan,
referring to the careful attention she paid Carrington after
Strachey's death, "I've been mistaken about Virginia; somewhere she keeps a warm heart" (Holroyd 691).

Could it be, then, that one definition of Modernism
should underscore the momentary, deliberate, and often
ultimate eruption of an overtly homoerotic—yet (*pace*
Sedgwick) covertly feminocentric—sentimentality all the

more powerful ("potent, symptomatic, and, perhaps, friable or volatile") for its unexpected inclusion in an otherwise ironic text? And that, not so contrary to popular belief, modern irony should be read as inauthentic, modern sentimentality as real? Certainly, the case can be made. One need only consider such sentimental moments as Frédéric Moreau telling his friend Deslauriers in *Sentimental Education* (1869) that the time they *didn't* make it to the brothel "was the happiest time we ever had" (419) (distressed young men in the foreground, young women— prostitutes—in the background), or Stephen Dedalus in *Ulysses* (1922) finding his little sister Dilly with a French primer and realizing he can't save her (distressed young man in the foreground, young woman in the background). But it's more complicated than that. Consider, for instance, the sentimental moment in "Repeat After Me" when Lisa tells her brother about the accident and then falls apart: distressed young woman in the foreground (Lisa), young man in the background (Sedaris). Or the moment when Salinger's Zooey Glass does save his sister Franny by explaining who their brother Seymour's Fat Lady really is— the one for whom Zooey used to shine his unseen shoes and Franny, thinking the lady has cancer, tried to be funny: distressed young woman in the foreground (Franny), dead young man in the background (Seymour the suicide), distressed old woman behind him (the Fat Lady), and even older dead young man—"Christ Himself"—behind her. Fortunately, another Fat Lady (for she's come out that way), another *cancer-ridden* Fat Lady (she's come out that way as well) can help us understand such a moment, in part by having acted as an aloof scrutineer of her own public, overtly homoerotic, yet—truth be told—covertly feminocentric sentimentality. No, not Sharon. ("It's fat, my ass, but not as big as the can on that prize heifer" ["Get Your Ya-Ya's Out!" 32].) Eve.

Although I'm not sure any gay men identify with *her,*
Eve Kosofsky Sedgwick, a self-proclaimed "pervert" others
see as straight, does identify with us—a function of her
anal eroticism as well as of our having occupied analogous
closets. She also identifies with dying gay men—a function of her having confused breast cancer with AIDS. And
while she's quite sorry for ones who have died young,
whether of AIDS, at the hands of gay-bashers, or through
suicide—Sedgwick's public writing about them is far more
sentimental than deconstructive criticism had ever allowed
itself to be—her most interesting ("potent, symptomatic,
and, perhaps, friable or volatile") sentimental (or *peri-*
sentimental) moment concerns a distressed young woman
(Eve Kosofsky) and the older young woman (Queen Esther)
behind her. Or rather, the Eve behind the Esther. (It's
another public moment. I'm in no position to comment on
Sedgwick's private sentimentality—on her very "being."
I only know "Eve Sedgwick." But nor am I in a position
to argue that the private sentimentality of someone like
Sedgwick—a category that does include me—is any different from, or realer than, her public.)

Unbeknownst to the author herself (or so it would
appear), Sedgwick indicates an identification with Racine's
"salvific" heroine early on in *Epistemology of the Closet*
(1990). "Even today," she says in a parenthetical aside,
"Jewish little girls are educated in gender roles—fondness for being looked at, fearlessness in defense of 'their
people,' nonsolidarity with their sex—through masquer-
ading as Queen Esther at Purim; I have a snapshot of
myself at about five, barefoot in the pretty 'Queen Esther'
dress my grandmother made (white satin, gold spangles),
making a careful eyes-down toe-pointed curtsey at (presumably) my father, who is manifest in the picture only as
the flashgun that hurls my shadow, pillaring up tall and
black, over the dwarfed sofa onto the wall behind me" (82).

Later on, in an aside that explicates a decision "to break
with the tradition of personal disclaimer and touch ground
myself with a rapid but none the less genuine guilty plea
to possessing the attributes, in a high degree, of at the
very least sentimentality, prurience, and morbidity" (153),
Sedgwick acknowledges this identification—an identification, I hasten to add, that has nothing to do with self-pity:

> On the infinitesimally small chance that any
> skepticism could greet this confession, I can offer
> as evidence of liability—or, one might say, of
> expert qualification—the pathos injected in the
> paraphrase of *Esther,* in Chapter 1, which I loved
> composing but which is rendered both creepy and,
> perhaps, rhetorically efficacious by a certain
> obliquity in my own trail of identifications. As a
> friend who disliked those paragraphs put it acidly,
> it's not me risking the coming out, but it's all too
> visibly me having the salvational fantasies.
> (153–54)

So it turns out that Sedgwick's identifications with
both gay men and Queen Esther are not very different
from Woolf's identifications with Strachey and Carrington. It also turns out that postmodern criticism—or queer
theory, at any rate (thanks, in large part, to Sedgwick)—
was more capable than modern literature of comprehend-
ing (both willing to deploy and able to fathom) sentimentality. But what about that "thanks"? What is it about
Sedgwick that made so many of us want to please her—
and even, with all due aggression, to imitate her? (What
was it about Sharon? What about Sedaris?) She seems to
think she's a mother figure, or in other words that we
all wrote *Remembrance of Things Past.* ("Is it not the
mother to whom both the coming-out testament and its
continued refusal to come out are addressed? And isn't

some scene like that behind the persistent force of the novel's trope, 'the profanation of the mother'?" Sedgwick asks. The answer is yes, of course. This topos of the omnipotent, unknowing mother, moreover, "is profoundly rooted in twentieth-century gay male high culture, along the whole spectrum from Pasolini to David Leavitt, by way of, for instance, James Merrill" [248–49]. Then again, Sedgwick can imagine *herself* as Proust as well: "Who hasn't dreamt that *A la recherche* remained untranslated, simply so that one could (at least if one knew French) by undertaking the job justify spending one's own productive life afloat within that blissful and hilarious atmosphere of truth-telling" [240].) She's also a kind of fag hag, to use the horrible expression Sedgwick herself disavows. I myself have already argued elsewhere that she's a diva. But, as you may have guessed by now, I also think she'd become our own Fat Lady (if not Christ Himself), someone we were supposed to do all sorts of things for (shine those shoes, try to be funny, be *sentimental*)—and that she'd become her for reasons that reflect Sedgwick's own feminocentric sentimentality. After all, the woman was dying. She may even—like Sharon—be dead by the time you read this. As may I. Yet unlike Salinger's basically pathetic figure, Sedgwick—like Sharon—seemed ideal as well. To be so bold as to invoke Strachey's sentimentality—and without any irony I can detect, not to mention any barely sublimated sexual feelings—she was a crusty, sublime, devastating, and terrific old *woman.*

But what if our sentimentality *is,* if not excessive, inauthentic? To pose a series of naive and somewhat disingenuous questions, what if some of us *do* turn it off and on like charm? (Or like sarcasm.) What if, for some of us, sentimentality *is* our particular charm? (Must one, for example, have a heart of stone to read *Beethoven's Kiss* without laughing?) Do we turn it on simply because (yet

how complicated that "simply" is), as writers who've confused the emotion with pity, we need readers to *love* us?
(Readers like Sedgwick, that is. Or Sharon. Or Sam.) And
to re-pose the final question of Wilde's *An Ideal Husband,*
the oddest (most potent, symptomatic, friable and volatile)
of the plays: "Is it love you feel for me, or is it pity merely?"

Works by David Sedaris

Barrel Fever (Boston: Little, Brown, 1994)
- "Parade"
- "Music for Lovers"
- "The Last You'll Hear from Me"
- "My Manuscript"
- "Firestone"
- "We Get Along"
- "Glen's Homophobia Newsletter Vol. 3, No. 2"
- "Don's Story"
- "Season's Greetings to Our Friends and Family!!!"
- "Jamboree"
- "After Malison"
- "Barrel Fever"
- "Diary of a Smoker"
- "Giantess"
- "The Curly Kind"
- "SantaLand Diaries"

Naked (Boston: Little, Brown, 1997)
    "Chipped Beef"
    "A Plague of Tics"
    "Get Your Ya-Ya's Out!"
    "Next of Kin"
    "Cyclops"
    "The Women's Open"
    "True Detective"
    "Dix Hill"
    "I Like Guys"
    "The Drama Bug"
    "Dinah, the Christmas Whore"
    "Planet of the Apes"
    "The Incomplete Quad"
    "C.O.G."
    "Something for Everyone"
    "Ashes"
    "Naked"

Holidays on Ice (Boston: Little, Brown, 1997)
    "SantaLand Diaries"
    "Season's Greetings to Our Friends and Family!!!"
    "Dinah, the Christmas Whore"
    "Front Row Center with Thaddeus Bristol"
    "Based Upon a True Story"
    "Christmas Means Giving"

Me Talk Pretty One Day (Boston: Little, Brown, 2000)
    "Go Carolina"
    "Giant Dreams, Midget Abilities"
    "Genetic Engineering"
    "Twelve Moments in the Life of the Artist"
    "You Can't Kill the Rooster"
    "The Youth in Asia"
    "The Learning Curve"

"Big Boy"
"The Great Leap Forward"
"Today's Special"
"City of Angels"
"A Shiner Like a Diamond"
"Nutcracker.com"
"See You Again Yesterday"
"Me Talk Pretty One Day"
"Jesus Shaves"
"The Tapeworm Is In"
"Make That a Double"
"Remembering My Childhood on the Continent of
     Africa"
"21 Down"
"The City of Light in the Dark"
"I Pledge Allegiance to the Bag"
"Picka Pocketoni"
"I Almost Saw This Girl Get Killed"
"Smart Guy"
"The Late Show"
"I'll Eat What He's Wearing"

Dress Your Family in Corduroy and Denim (Boston:
Little, Brown, 2004)
"Us and Them"
"Let It Snow"
"The Ship Shape"
"Full House"
"Consider the Stars"
"Monie Changes Everything"
"The Change in Me"
"Hejira"
"Slumus Lordicus"
"The Girl Next Door"
"Blood Work"

"The End of the Affair"
"Repeat After Me"
"Six to Eight Black Men"
"Rooster at the Hitchin' Post"
"Possession"
"Put a Lid on It"
"A Can of Worms"
"Chicken in the Henhouse"
"Who's the Chef?"
"Baby Einstein"
"Nuit of the Living Dead"

References

Barthes, Roland. *A Lover's Discourse: Fragments*. Trans. Richard Howard. New York: Hill & Wang, 1978.

———. *"Longtemps, je me suis couché de bonne heure . . ."* The *Rustle of Language*. Trans. Richard Howard. 277–90. New York: Hill & Wang, 1986.

Benjamin, Walter. "The Image of Proust." *Illuminations: Essays and Reflections*. Ed. Hannah Arendt. Trans. Harry Zohn. 201–15. New York: Schocken, 1985 [1929].

Berger, John. *Ways of Seeing*. London: Penguin, 1972.

Bersani, Leo. "Is the Rectum a Grave?" *October* 43 (Winter 1987): 197–222.

de Man, Paul. *Allegories of Reading: Figural Language in Rousseau, Nietzsche, Rilke, and Proust*. New Haven, Conn.: Yale University Press, 1979.

Donne, John. *Sermons*. 10 vols. Ed. George Potter and Evelyn Simpson. Berkeley: University of California Press, 1953–62 [1640–60].

Dujardin, Mireille. *Les Dentellières lesbiennes au moyen-âge*. Archives Nationales, Paris.

Flaubert, Gustave. *Sentimental Education*. Trans. Robert Baldick. Harmondsworth: Penguin, 1964 [1869].

Genette, Gérard. *Narrative Discourse: An Essay in Method.* Trans. Jane E. Lewin. Ithaca, N.Y.: Cornell University Press, 1980.

Gide, André. *The Immoralist.* Trans. Richard Howard. New York: Vintage, 1996 [1921].

Goodkin, Richard E. *Around Proust.* Princeton, N.J.: Princeton University Press, 1991.

Griffin, Dustin H. *Satire: A Critical Reintroduction.* Lexington: University Press of Kentucky, 1994.

Highet, Gilbert. *The Anatomy of Satire.* Princeton, N.J.: Princeton University Press, 1962.

Holroyd, Michael. *Lytton Strachey: The New Biography.* New York: Farrar, Strauss, and Giroux, 1994.

Johnson, Samuel. *Dr. Johnson's Critical Vocabulary: A Selection from His Dictionary.* Ed. Richard L. Harp. New York: University Press of America, 1986 [1755].

King, Florence. *Confessions of a Failed Southern Lady.* New York: St. Martin's Press, 1990.

Koestenbaum, Wayne. "Logorrhea." *Southwest Review* 79.1 (Winter 1994): 102–6.

Kopelson, Kevin. *Love's Litany: The Writing of Modern Homoerotics.* Stanford, Calif.: Stanford University Press, 1994.

Kramer, Lawrence. *After the Lovedeath: Sexual Violence and the Making of Culture.* Berkeley: University of California Press, 1997.

Ladenson, Elisabeth. *Proust's Lesbianism.* Ithaca, N.Y.: Cornell University Press, 1999.

La Rochefoucauld, François, Duc de. *Maxims.* Trans. Leonard Tancock. London: Penguin, 1959 [1665–94].

Miller, D. A. *Jane Austen, or The Secret of Style.* Princeton, N.J.: Princeton University Press, 2003.

———. *Place for Us: Essay on the Broadway Musical.* Cambridge, Mass.: Harvard University Press, 1998.

Nabokov, Vladimir. *Lolita.* New York: Putnam, 1955.

Nietzsche, Friedrich. *The Gay Science.* Trans. Josefine Nauckhoff. Cambridge: Cambridge University Press, 2001 [1882–87].

———. *Human, All Too Human.* Trans. R. J. Hollingdale. Cambridge: Cambridge University Press, 1996 [1878–86].

———. *Untimely Meditations*. Trans. R. J. Hollingdale. Cambridge: Cambridge University Press, 1997 [1873–76].

Painter, George D. *Marcel Proust: A Biography*. 2 vols. New York: Vintage, 1978.

Probyn, Elspeth. *Blush: Faces of Shame*. Minneapolis: University of Minnesota Press, 2005.

Proust, Marcel. *In Search of Lost Time*. 6 vols. Trans. C. K. Scott Moncrieff and Terence Kilmartin. Revised by D. J. Enright. New York: Modern Library, 1992 [1913–27].

Salinger, J. D. *Raise High the Roof Beam, Carpenters and Seymour: An Introduction*. Boston: Little, Brown, 1963 [1955; 1959].

Sedaris, David, ed. *Children Playing before a Statue of Hercules*. New York: Simon & Schuster, 2005.

Sedgwick, Eve Kosofsky. *Epistemology of the Closet*. Berkeley: University of California Press, 1990.

Strachey, Lytton. *Eminent Victorians*. New York: Harcourt, n.d. [1918].

Svevo, Italo. *Confessions of Zeno*. Trans. Beryl de Zoete. New York: Vintage, 1989 [1923].

Tadié, Jean-Yves. *Marcel Proust: A Life*. Trans. Euan Cameron. New York: Viking, 2000.

Woolf, Virginia. *Jacob's Room*. London: Penguin, 1992 [1922].

Kevin Kopelson is professor of English at the University of Iowa and author of *Neatness Counts: Essays on the Writer's Desk* (Minnesota, 2004). His other books include *Love's Litany, Beethoven's Kiss,* and *The Queer Afterlife of Vaslav Nijinsky.*